2020 Election Candidates & Issues

A look at the 2020 Presidential Race

R. Frederick Riddle

Printed by Kindle Direct Publishing, a registered trademark of Amazon.com

Published by T&R Independent Books, Port Charlotte, Florida an independent publisher.

This is a work drawn on publicly available information and represents the author's opinion based on that information. The opinions stated in this book are the author's unless otherwise stated.

ISBN- 9781686577765

Printed by Kindle Direct Publishing, a registered trademark of Amazon.com

Published by T&R Independent Books, Port Charlotte, Florida an independent publisher.

This is a work drawn on publicly available information and represents the author's opinion based on that information. The opinions stated in this book are the author's unless otherwise stated.

ISBN- 9781686577765

T&R
Independent Books

DEDICATION PAGE

This book is written with a desire to inform the American public on the candidates, their experience, beliefs, and record. In addition, this book covers important information regarding our government and other issues.

R. Frederick Riddle

Note from the author . . .

I'm a relic.

That's right. I grew up when Democrats and Republicans had civil disagreements that could be discussed without personal attacks or disparagement.

I believe the current state of uncivil discussion is not healthy for our nation we love. Whether you believe it started with the Democrats during Reagan's Presidency (as I do) or with the Republicans under President George Bush (as Democrats seem to) it affects both parties and endangers the American Representative Democracy that has served us so well.

(Quick quiz: When were we a democracy and how long did it last?

Answer: We have never been a democracy. See Chapter Thirty-One.)

We are now approaching the 2020 election with stark contrasts between Democrats and Republicans. It comes at a time when America has moved further to the right.

Which way will America turn next? This book seeks to inform you about each candidate that is running. The author is himself a conservative, but I've tried to present a balanced picture concerning each candidate.

I've also included my own analysis plus Author Notes which admittedly comes from a conservative position. But I've drawn information from other sources to be as honest and forthright as possible.

But it remains every American citizen's responsibility to determine the man or woman we want to lead this nation for the next four years. It's not only important for us but for our children, grandchildren, and the world.

R. Frederick Riddle

Contents

ONE : INTRODUCTION

As we approach the 2020 election, we find many Democratic candidates running for the Presidency of the United States. Why so many?

That's a good question and in this chapter, I will attempt to bring some understanding.

In 2016 most of the media, including the so-called prognosticators, thought that Hillary Clinton would win the election. Donald Trump was merely an interesting and bombastic opponent who didn't have a chance.

To back up this image the Democratic Party and the news media heavily relied upon the various polls that predicted a Hillary election. The problem was that these polls were wrong, in part because they included non-citizens and non-voting people in their polling data.

To my knowledge there was only one that predicted a Trump win and it was based on grassroots polling. What the pollsters didn't see or want to see was that the American people's mood had shifted. Normally center right, it had moved further right in some of its political beliefs and aspirations. In short, the American people were more populist than either Democrats or Republicans.

In conjunction with this the people had moved to the right and were more Republican than Democrat in their thinking. And in a country where the liberals had control of states with large populations and thereby arguably most of the people in the United States, such as New York and California, they thought they were in a good position.

They forgot that we are not and never were a democracy but rather a Representative Democracy. The number of people voting for a candidate in a national election is interesting, but it is who wins the most states with the most electoral votes. And the race was lost in the populist states that lay between New York and California.

When they lost the election on November 8, 2016, they made a fatal mistake. Instead of recognizing their weaknesses and targeting them for revamping, they blamed their loss on a fake collusion charge. They demanded and got a Special Counsel to investigate this bogus charge and for two years have promised the American people that the investigation would bring down President Trump.

We know how that worked out.

Fast forward to 2019 and we see the Democratic Party still in denial, still claiming collusion, and still trying to undermine the President. This has won them accolades from the Press and from their core followers, but President Trump has seen his personal popularity rise and the approval rating is in the 50s percentile.

Another factor that cannot be ignored has been the childish actions of the Democrats, especially in the House. They took over in the 2018 mid-term election and immediately touted the Blue Wave.

Unfortunately for them the Blue Wave never happened. Yes, they took the House back. But this is not uncommon in mid-term elections. From the beginning it looked like the Republicans would lose seats (primarily because once in power they reneged on promises they'd made while Democrats were in power). But a Blue Wave would have taken both the House and the Senate!

Instead of losing the Senate, the Republicans increased their control of the Senate! That was huge! So instead of a Blue Wave we saw a surge of Republicans in the Senate race. It wasn't a Red Wave because they lost the House, but it was impressive.

Now of course there are voices in the House calling for impeachment of the President. Some of the leaders recognize this as a mistake, but the noisy few are adamant. All of this has laid a foundation for the coming election.

There is very little if any mystery concerning the Republican Party. While there is one opponent it is my belief, they will nominate President Donald Trump for re-election. And they have a slew of reasons for thinking that it will happen.

Below is a partial list of his accomplishments despite a largely uncooperative House.

- Unraveled the rules that prevented small and medium-sized companies (including mom and pop) from starting and growing.

This red tape had grown over several years under President Obama and maybe even earlier.

- Canceled or withdrew from treaties that were contrary to American interests.
- Forced Europe to contribute more money and men to NATO.
- Appointed two new Conservative Supreme Court Judges.
- Appointed many Conservative judges throughout the judicial system.
- Moved our embassy to Jerusalem without the catastrophic results predicted.
- Brokered a deal with both Mexico and Canada.
- Inspired the economic boom (began under Obama after Trump's election and inspired by Trump's election).
- Has been tougher on Russia than his predecessor.
- Has been tougher on China than his predecessor.
- Has brought back prayer into government.
- Opened the door to Christianity.
- Black unemployment lowest in decades.
- Hispanic unemployment lowest in decades.
- Real jobs constantly being created.

While the press has tried to ignore these accomplishments, the American people are very much aware of them. That awareness has even been detected by the general polls but not to the actual degree, which is a rather common failure.

So, the President is shall we say, 'riding high'. In combination with his popularity is the unpopularity of the Mueller Investigation. Even the local and national press touched on the abusive tactics that Mueller used. However, while they only brushed the sides of that issue and revealed this behavior, they rarely investigated any of the resulting and, in my opinion, alarming issues.

One of the more interesting facets of the Mueller Investigation has been the trashing of his report and Attorney General William Barr's handling of the report by the left.

Mueller's Report has been trashed because he didn't arrive at the conclusions the Democrats wanted and needed. It left them hanging and they lashed out at him.

As for Barr's actions he went far beyond what he was required to do in revealing the report. According to snippets of information leaked out he only redacted those items required by law and demanded by constituted authorities. Congress received the most transparent document as was possible. But the problem was that it still didn't point to collusion on the part of Trump and the Russians.

So now the House is barking up the Obstruction of Justice tree. The problem here is there is even less evidence to support them. One question they should be required to answer is simply, how can there be obstruction of justice when no crime was found? How can you obstruct something that doesn't exist?

The American people have been watching this and will decide in 2020 the way forward. In the following alphabetical candidate profiles, I will explore their lives and electability.

Terms and Structure of this Book

Structure

Chapters : Except for the case of President Trump all candidates are listed in alphabetical order. Although there will be some differences I have included: Picture, basic Summary Facts, Biography, Career, Issues, My Analysis, and My Prediction.

In the Summary of Facts, I list several important information pertaining to the candidates service, education, website, politics, and ranking.

In the case of the Democrats (there are only two Republicans) I list their party as Democrat and their leaning as Moderately Left and Far Left.

This is primarily my take on their politics. While Biden comes the closest to a true moderate (aka centrist), even he has moved to the left so there are no true moderates running for the Democratic Party Nomination. I think it could be truly said that the Democratic Party is no longer the party of John F. Kennedy. I'm not sure he'd recognize the party at all!

Terms

In the Summary of Facts, I have included two ranking Terms.

Moderately Left

This describes the political leanings of a politician that is Left but doesn't support Medicare-for-All. When you examine all the candidates there is little that separates them. In many cases this is the only issue that divides them. They march in lockstep on almost all other issues with slightly different views, but otherwise the same.

In contrast the Far Left represents those candidates who are at the extreme left of the political spectrum. The defining issue is Medicare-for-All. Some of the Moderately Left politicians identify closely with the Far Left but haven't endorsed or fully endorsed the Medicare-for-All. Medicare-for-All with a public option is one such view that is very close but different.

You may use different litmus tests, but I chose the Medicare-for-All issue because it is so extreme and doesn't consider its high cost to the taxpayers (that's you and me). Other than that issue, most of them are alike in their preferences.

Don't be fooled by the media description of moderates. As stated previously Biden comes the closest to being identified as a moderate, but he has and is shifting his political stances to the left making him Moderately Left. I wouldn't be surprised if he eventually moves to the Far Left to protect his chances for the nomination. He wants to win badly and is not interested in a secondary role.

The first is called Name Recognition. This by its very nature is an arbitrary decision, since a candidate may be well known in his or her state but unknown elsewhere. I use national awareness which sometimes may mean that I had little or no awareness of them before writing this book.

The second ranking is called RealClearPolitics. I either use a number between 1 and 12 or I use 'N/R' for Not Relevant. While there is some arbitrariness involved, I base my decisions on the RealClearPolitics which is constantly changing and being updated.

On the next page are the top seven ranked candidates as of the publishing date plus a listing of sources used.

REALCLEARPOLITICS RANKING

Rank	Candidate	Date
1	Biden	08/16/2019
2	Warren	"
3	Sanders	"
4	Harris	"
5	Buttigieg	"
6	O'Rourke +	"
7	Booker +	"

This ranking is constantly changing. I don't vouch for its accuracy (see the chapter on Polls). But it at least gives you a glimpse of the possibilities.

The '+' sign means candidate moved up since last look; a '-' means the candidate moved down.

SOURCES USED FOR THIS BOOK

1. Campaign Websites
2. Mike Huckabee
3. Dick Morris
4. News media
5. Politico
6. RealClearPolitics
7. Wikipedia

TWO : BENNET

Michael Bennet

Summary of Facts

U.S. Senate Colorado

Party: Democrat

Tenure : 2009 - Present

Term ends : 2023

Years in position : 10

Compensation Base salary $174,000
Net worth (2015) $16,000,000
Last elected November 8, 2016
Appointed January 22, 2009
Education : Bachelor's Wesleyan University, Yale Law School
Campaign Website: michaelbennet.com
Political Leanings: Democrat; Moderately Left
Name Recognition: Poor
RealClearPolitics Poll: N/R

Biography
   Michael Bennet (born on November 28, 1964, in New Delhi, India) is
a Democratic member of the U.S. Senate from the state of Colorado. On

May 2, 2019, Bennet announced he was running for president of the United States. Thus, he joined the ever-growing list of candidates for the Presidency.

Bennet said his presidential campaign would focus on expanding economic opportunity and promoting integrity in government. As his campaign progresses, he will be expected to expand and detail just what he means. If he hopes to win the nomination, he will need to go further left than he currently appears to be.

Bennet was born in New Delhi, India, the son of Douglas (aid to Ambassador Chester Bowles) and Susanne. His father is a Christian and his mother a Jewish survivor of the Jewish Holocaust.

His family has a history of serving in government. His father ran the U.S. Agency for International Development under President Carter and Assistant Secretary of State for International Organization Affairs under President Clinton. Going further back, his grandfather, Douglas Bennet, was an economic adviser in President Franklin D. Roosevelt's administration.

Growing up, he spent most of his childhood in Washington, D.C. Because of dyslexia he was held back in the second grade yet went on to grow up and serve as a page on Capitol Hill.

Career

In 2009 the Governor of Colorado Bill Ritter (D) appointed Michael Bennet to the Senate to replace Ken Salazar (D) who'd become President Obama's Secretary of the Interior. Bennet not only finished the term, but he went on to win his first full term as a Senator in 2010 in a win over his Republican opponent Ken Buck by less than 2 percentage points. Later he was re-elected in 2016 over Darryl Glenn (R) by almost 6 percentage points.

Prior to his appointment as a Senator he served as chief of staff for Denver's Mayor John Hickenlooper from 2003 to 2005. Afterward he served as superintendent for Denver Public Schools from 2005 to 2009.

Below is a small capsule representing his political career as listed on the Internet. I've selected facts I believe are most relevant as his campaign begins.

- 2009-Present: U.S. Senator from Colorado
- 2005-2009: Superintendent, Denver Public Schools
- 2003-2005: Chief of staff to mayor of Denver
- 1997: Special assistant to U.S. attorney, Conn.
- 1995-1997: Counsel to U.S. deputy attorney general
- 1993: Graduated from Yale Law School with J.D.
- 1987: Graduated from Wesleyan University with B.A.

The senator is considered an average Democratic member of Congress who votes with the party on most bills (ranked in 2014 as 93.8%). His votes tend to align with Charles Schumer (D) and Susan Collins (R). Likely he is Center Left in his political stance.

Since becoming a Senator, Bennet has served on several committees. Here is just a partial listing of the committees:

- Committee on Intelligence (Select) (2019-2020)
- Committee on Agriculture, Nutrition and Forestry Members (2011-2020)
- Committee on Finance (2013-2020)
- Committee on Health, Education, Labor, and Pensions
- Banking, Housing, and Urban Affairs
- Aging
- And related subcommittees

Aside from these assignments giving a wide platform of experience, he was also a member of the: **Gang of Eight.** This was in 2013 it consisted of four senators from each party. The group proposed comprehensive and bipartisan legislation concerning the immigration issue.

There were the 'four basic pillars' that the Gang of Eight embraced and pursued:

1) A "tough but fair path to citizenship . . . .contingent upon securing our borders and tracking whether legal immigrants have left the country as required";
2) Reform our legal immigration system with a greater eye toward our economic needs;
3) Workplace verification; and
4) Setting up of a system for admitting future workers into America (although the term "guest worker" is not used).

ISSUES

Abortion

No Policy Statements

Agriculture

- Supports the Dairy Margin program for farmers

Climate Change

- Supports tax credits for solar manufacturing
- Supported the Keystone XL pipeline
- Supports the Clean Power Plan

Criminal Justice Reform

- No Policy Statements

Economy

- No Policy Statements

Education

- No Policy Statements

Election Reform

- No Policy Statements

Foreign Relations

- Opposes war in Yemen
- Alarmed about China's undue influence

Guns

- Supports stricter gun control
- Opposed the federal assault weapons ban

Healthcare

- Supported Affordable Care Act
- Supports Medicare X (Medicare-for-All with a public option)

Immigration

- Supported and cosponsored the 2009 DREAM ACT
- Supported as part of the Gang of Eight the Border Security, Economic Opportunity, and Immigration Modernization Act of 2013

LGBT

- Supports same-sex marriage

Marijuana

- Supported and cosponsored legislation exempting individuals or corporations from federal enforcement of Controlled Substances Act
- Supported SAFE Banking Act

My Analysis

You will have notice that there are several places where the phrase 'No policy statements' shows up. It is possible there has been expressed an opinion or stated policy on these issues and that I didn't see them. In which case I apologize for my failure. But as far as I know there has not been an opinion expressed on these issues.

Outside of Colorado Senator Bennet seems relatively unknown which creates an immediate problem for him. Name recognition is vital in both the Primary and the General Election. It is a monumental hill to climb.

That is not an easy task. But the truth of the matter is that he has time to do it. The Convention doesn't take place until 2020. A lot can happen during that time.

Electability

Senator Bennet has a small base to build upon within his own state. His record shows that the people of Colorado like him. That would seem to be a major Plus for him. It will be interesting to see how he fares within his own state against the behemoths like Biden and Sanders.

But carrying your own state, while important, is not enough. He must have appeal throughout the United States. That means having a clear, understandable, and embraceable position on subjects like the economy, international relations, military preparedness, and immigration.

His voting record indicates that he votes with the Democratic majority most of the time, which should win approval of the Democratic voters. But the key here to me is that this voting record was accomplished prior to the Party's further leftward move. Having looked at his record it appears he has the leftist credentials to identify and maybe attract the Party's base. However, I believe he represents the Moderately Left (as there is no true Moderate Candidate, which would be more centrist).

Originally, I didn't think he was far enough to the left to be a serious contender, but after reading his record I have arrived at a far different conclusion. But is he far enough to the Left to be a factor? A lot will depend on what he does in the debates.

My Prediction

Bennet is an interesting candidate. As mentioned above he fits into the left mold of the Democratic Party. Is he far enough left?

There is a possibility that while he is not as far left as the Party has gone the voters within the Party may view him as a compromise. He's left and yet he may by personality appear more reasonable than others thereby being more electable.

However so far, he hasn't shown the ability to step out of the pack. In fact, his RealClearPolitics rating is so far back it's not relevant. If he is to move forward and contend for the nomination, he needs to take a stand.

This will be hard since so many of the candidates take such similar stances as he does. He must find a way to stand out from the pack and so far, he hasn't been able to do so.

Now, I consider him to be a Dark Horse for the nomination. But that's on the assumption he steps his game up. Failure to do that will quickly diminish his candidacy. I am currently giving him the benefit of doubt and saying he will last until Super Tuesday.

However, if he fails to garner enough votes to put himself into the mix, I think he will drop out soon after Super Tuesday.

What if his candidacy takes off?

Such an even would certainly make the primary more interesting. But he has one failing mark that I think will defeat him. In this year of the woman he is not a woman!

With that in mind, I think he drops out after Super Tuesday. He might also be a dark horse to win the nomination. If he wins, he will not beat Trump for the same reason I've given for others: The Democratic Party has moved too far left and is not in contact with real America which is basically Center-Right.

THREE : BIDEN

Joe Biden

Summary of Facts

Former
U.S. Vice President

Party: Democrat

Tenure : 2009 - 2017

Years in position : 8

Compensation Base salary $
Net worth (2018) $ 15,600,000
Last elected : 2012
Campaign Website: https://joebiden.com/
Political Leanings: Democrat; Moderately Left
Name Recognition: Great
RealClearPolitics Poll: 01

Biography

Prior to serving as Vice President of the United States, Joe Biden represented Delaware as a U.S. Senator from 1973 to 2009. During his time in the Senate he served on and chaired the Senate Judiciary Committee and the Senate Foreign Relations Committee for several years.

In 2008 then Senator Biden was selected by the Democratic Candidate for President Barack Obama to be his running mate. In November the team won the election beating John McClain and Sarah Palin. With that win Senator Biden became Vice President Biden.

He has had a long career that spanned over three decades in the Senate and eight years as Vice President. While a liberal, his service has primarily been more center left than left. In my opinion he will be judged a good senator.

Career
Senator from Delaware 1973-2009
Vice President of U.S. 2009-2017

Bad News for Biden

On March 29, 2019 Lucy Flores, who ran for Lieutenant Governor of Nevada in 2014, dropped a bombshell. She wrote an essay that appeared in *The Cut* that she'd been inappropriately touched by Biden during a campaign stop.

Biden got out in front of the allegation and said the following, "In many years on the campaign trail and in public life, I have offered countless handshakes, hugs, expressions of affection, support and comfort. And not once — never — did I believe I acted inappropriately. If it is suggested that I did so I will listen respectfully. But it was never my intention."

Whatever the truth it probably hurt his campaign and gave it a rough start. It didn't help that six more women also said they had inappropriate interactions with Biden. These included prolonged hugs and touching that extended over a week.

(Authors note: It is difficult to determine the truthfulness of such allegations so many years *after* the supposed act was to have occurred. It is a case of he said/she said and if you're politically correct, you'll side with 'she said'. That sounds too much like the #MeToo movement which only requires an allegation not proof. But that is the world we live in today; instead of being considered innocent until proven guilty you're guilty until proven innocent. This is a long way from the America our forefathers founded!)

This resulted in a Biden tweet, "Social norms are changing. I understand that, and I've heard what these women are saying. Politics to me has always been about making connections, but I will be more mindful about respecting personal space in the future. That's my responsibility and I will meet it."

Is it enough? We'll see.

The verdict didn't take long in coming, however. Other candidates criticized his apology, some characterizing it as either not good enough or as being too late. This has the sense of a long running problem for the senator.

If that wasn't enough, he performed a classic flip-flop this past June.

Earlier in June he came out and restated his support for the Hyde Amendment. For those who don't know what the Hyde Amendment is, let me explain.

The Hyde Amendment bans Medicaid coverage for abortion. This is an issue that cuts right to the core of the Far Left. They believe that abortion is a right and should be covered by insurance, including Medicaid.

A week later Biden performed a flip-flop and swore fealty to opposing the Hyde Amendment. This is a serious injury that his campaign has suffered. When combined with troubles with inappropriate touching it could derail him entirely.

Then there is the matter of his record. Although no-one would ever mistake him for a conservative, he has taken conservative positions over his thirty-six-year career.

These include support for capital punishment, against legalization of marijuana, opposed to Medicare-for-All, and against gay marriage. Add to this his support of the Iraq War, NAFTA, Pacific Rim Treaty, and Welfare reform (contrary to far-left sentiments) may well put his campaign on life support.

It raises the issue of just who is Joe Biden. What does he believe? Can he be trusted? It may not be asked like that, but I believe that those are underlining questions that ultimately could undermine any chance he has to become President.

If I was a rival I'd be publicly asking, "Does Joe really believe that or is he saying it to get your votes?" It's a question he might have trouble answering.

As the Primary season continues forward, I would not be surprised to hear his rivals, particularly those candidates closest to him in the rankings, taking aim at his past positions and any new positions he assumes. In fact, it is already happening as his substantial lead has continually been losing ground.

And waiting in the wings are other aspirants, especially Elizabeth Warren and Kamala Harris. These two Far Right candidates are taking center stage.

ISSUES

Abortion
- No Policy Statements

Climate Change
- Supports investing in clean energy
- Supports rolling back the Trump tax incentives to pay for investments

Criminal Justice Reform
- No Policy Statements

Economy
- Supports Minimum Wage: $15 an hour

Education
- Supports our educators by giving them the pay and dignity they deserve.
- Invest in resources for our schools so students grow into physically and emotionally healthy adults, and educators can focus on teaching.
- Ensure that no child's future is determined by their zip code, parents' income, race, or disability.
- Provide every middle and high school student a path to a successful career.
- Start investing in our children at birth.

Election Reform
- No Policy Statements

Foreign Relations
- No Policy Statements

Guns
- No Policy Statements

Healthcare
- Supports Affordable Health Care

Immigration
- Supports adequate funding for Border Patrol

LGBT
- No Policy Statements

Marijuana
- No Policy Statements

Reparations
- No Policy Statements

My Analysis

Joe Biden is a very effective debater. He has served in the U.S. Senate for 36 years and has been a steadfast liberal throughout his political history. However, he has now found out that he is more center left than he is outright left which puts him at odds with both the Democratic base which is Far-Left and America which is Center Right. Although he got off to an early lead in the running for President, I believe it is unlikely he'll win the primary.

Why?

He won't win the primary because he's simply not left enough. He'd have to significantly change his views on several issues to accomplish that miracle. It would do violence to his stands he's embraced over the years. Difficult, but not impossible.

[Author's Note: And as pointed out above it would put his honesty and dependability in question.]

That's not to say he won't attempt such a departure, but if he does his opponents will certainly point out to the voters his switch. In fact, he has been trying to mend his fences and move further left already and has already been rebuffed. If the preceding continues his campaign will eventually stall. (As pointed out above there is evidence that such a stall is already occurring.)

He does have some weaknesses. For example, he professes support for teachers and claims that teachers haven't received a wage increase since 1996. So where was he as Senator and Vice President? If he presses this issue people may ask hard questions.

He also supports Home Visits by government officials regarding health care. That form of government control may work for the Far Left, but for most Americans this could be a problem.

These are just two issues that could cause a problem for him. Another is the matter of tax incentives as seen in Author's Note. The American people have seen increased take home pay and many people previously unemployed have become employed, including blacks and Latinos.

These disparities between his rhetoric and existing facts indicate a disconnection with reality. True, most Democrats probably agree with him, but what about the Independents?

Another factor that has significant potential to undo his candidacy is the fake outrageous ire of his opponents over his working with men who were either members of the KKK or sympathizers. The problem is that Biden harkens back to the days when you worked with other politicians you may dislike or abhor so that you can achieve a desirable goal.

He did that and now the new moral is that such working together marks you a racist. He is not a racist, but a pragmatist (at least in this case) trying to achieve a political end. In today's political environment you can't do that. This cost him a lot of Black support.

As candidates go, he'd probably be the strongest opponent to President Trump, but would likely not prevail. Although the mass media continually compares the individual candidates against Trump and have them winning, that is because they use unreliable polling data, such as was used in 2016. (Most polls include more than likely voters; some include people residing in local cemeteries. Some Fact Checkers say this is untrue, but appearances can outweigh facts. See Chapter Thirty.)

One last point is that Biden is trying to update his Leftist credentials by attacking President Trump's rhetoric. His attack in August (Saying that President Trump has "fanned the flames of white supremacy in this nation," is both a false narrative and a risky effort to directly link the president to the mass shooting in El Paso, Texas.

My Prediction:

With all the baggage, earned and unearned, he's carrying, I suspect he'll withdraw sometime between Super Tuesday and the Democratic

National Convention. However, If the race is tight, I can see him fighting in the Convention itself for the nomination. If he does that and can open the Convention, he has a lot of political capital that could come into play.

But if he is perceived as waffling on the issues then his candidacy would be short-lived indeed. It doesn't help that he's shown signs of incoherency lately. It's another issue that could undo him.

The greater part is how would he fare against President Trump in the General Election? Going against a popular president is always tough, but when you don't know that he is popular (a common malady of Democrats) then the going can be very rough.

But assuming he faces Trump in the General Election the fight will be classic. On the Left you have the champion debater skilled in political strategies while on the Right you have the renowned Populist Businessman skilled in communicating to the common man and condensing complicated issues down to understandable and simple terms. It would go down as one of the greatest political contests in American history.

In such a battle Biden would have the edge in reaching those who consider themselves to be extremely intelligent and look down at the rest of the world. These are the makers and shakers of business and the media. He will also have backing him billions of dollars from the rich and famous. (Isn't it amazing that the Democratic Party, supposedly the Party of the little guy, draws much of its support from the rich and famous?)

But Trump will reach out to the common man with the simple yet effective message of let's 'Keep America Great Again'. It's a message that still rings in our hearts. I mentioned earlier that he can take complex theories and simplify them so that we can understand. It doesn't matter if it's not entirely accurate, what matters is that we are able to understand the issue in its simplest terms and thereby make decisions.

Trump has the entire history of America at his beck and call. He points to that history to provide us with an understanding of where we were and what we've become. The result is that while the media points out the smallest of mistakes the people can grasp the truth and run with it. This is a skill that Trump used in 2016 and will use in 2020 to great effect!

And when the dust is settled President Trump will emerge the champion!

You've already seen I'm a supporter of the President. I support him because he's what we need. In Chapter Thirty I go in depth on him and even spend time on why I support him.

The truth is that I am a Christian, a conservative, and a patriotic American. I am also deeply concerned about the future of America. On top of everything else I take note not so much of what his enemies say about him but what he does and says.

Biden seems to be an experienced politician, but that is part of the problem. Today his party has moved significantly to the left and values the principles of the left above experience. I don't think the Party will select him as the leader of the Party simply because he doesn't have the new credentials needed. While Biden has made small steps to accommodate them, he hasn't gone far enough to satisfy the new center of the party.

He withdraws sometime between Super Tuesday and the Democratic National Convention.

FOUR : de BLASIO

Bill de Blasio

Summary of Facts
Mayor of New York

Party: Democrat

Tenure : 2013 - Present

Term ends : 2021

Years in position : 5

Compensation Base salary $258,000
Net worth (2012) n/a
Last elected November 7, 2017
Education : New York University; Columbia University, Yale
Campaign Website: billdeblasio.com
Political Leanings: Democrat; Far Left
Name Recognition: Medium
RealClearPolitics Poll: N/R

Biography

Mayor de Blasio was born in New York City on May 8, 1961. He holds a B.A. from New York University and an M.A. from Columbia University's School of International and Public Affairs. At the age of 36 he became the Regional Director of the U.S. Department of Housing and Urban Development (1997-1998). In 1999 he served on the District 15's School

Board in Brooklyn. From there he moved up to the New York City Council District 39, serving from 2002 to 2009.

As Mayor he's made a name for himself that has given him name recognition far outside New York.

However, that name is not necessarily a positive feature. For instance, further down in this chapter you will read of his problems with the Police Department. Having low morale among the police who are charged with protecting the citizens is not a good thing. And there are a lot of people out there that have a deep respect for First Responders.

Mayor de Blasio has some bridge building to do. in fact, I came across some articles that question whether there is any real support out there for him.

Career
- 2013-Present: Mayor of New York
- 2010-2013: New York City Public Advocate
- 2002-2009: Member of the New York City Council, District 39
- 1999: Member of District 15's School Board in Brooklyn
- 1997-1998: Regional Director for the U.S. Department of Housing and Urban Development

ISSUES

Abortion
- Opposes Hyde Amendment

Climate Change
- No Policy Statements

Criminal Justice Reform
- Opposes Stop & Frisk
- Had bad relations with NYPD with many thinking of leaving department

Economy
- Raise the federal minimum wage, so that it reaches $15/hour, while indexing it to inflation.
- Reform the National Labor Relations Act, to enhance workers' right to organize and rebuild the middle class. Close the carried interest loophole.

- End tax breaks for companies that ship jobs overseas.
- Implement the "Buffett Rule" so millionaires pay their fair share.
- Close the CEO tax loophole that allows corporations to take advantage of "performance pay" write-offs
- Pass comprehensive immigration reform to grow the economy and protect against exploitation of low-wage workers.
- Oppose trade deals that hand more power to corporations at the expense of American jobs, workers' rights, and the environment.
- Invest in schools, not jails-- and give a second chance to those coming home from prison.
- Expand the Earned Income Tax Credit and protect and expand Social Security.

Education
- Pass national paid sick leave.
- Pass national paid family leave.
- Make Pre-K, after-school programs and childcare universal.
- Allow students to refinance student loan debt to take advantage of lower interest rates, and support debt-free college.
- College student loan debt forgiveness for veterans with disabilities.

Election Reform
- Supports abolishing the Electoral College
- Supports voting rights for all, including those incarcerated

Foreign Relations
- No Policy Statements

Guns
- Supports gun control

Healthcare
- Supports Medicare-for-All
- Supports ending private health insurance

Immigration
- Supports sanctuary cities

Marijuana
- Supports legalization of Marijuana

Reparations
Supports the idea of Reparations

My Analysis
Since Mayor Bill de Blasio took office, he has taken the city of New York several steps down the road to the extreme left. Some of his moves have been head scratchers at best. He's gotten into legislating what foods people can eat (undoubtedly to protect them). As questionable as these may seem it may have endeared him to the Far Left, which could carry him a long way into the Primary.

[Author's Note: Such decisions as mentioned above place him to the Far Left on the political scene. This places him at a good place in the Democratic Primary.]

His plan unveiled in 2015 came with no explanation of how he'd pay for it. As of this date I've been unable to find out what the costs and benefits have been of its implementation.

With the Mayor's activist approach, he hasn't shown much pull outside his own state. Nor have I heard of anyone taking him seriously (probably due to his war on bad food).

On top of all that, I believe that outside of New York his ideas will be largely rejected. Mid-America doesn't much care for the government running their lives.

Most Democrats seem agreeable to such overreaching but live in states like New York and California which are the largest in population. The problem for him is that there are other Far-Left candidates who will be appealing to the same constituents as he is trying to do. I think he will have a problem softening his public profile. His problems with the NYPD will not sell well in Mid-America. So, it remains to be seen what traction he gets.

As I searched for information upon de Blasio, I failed to find anything that would make him a desirable candidate. Obviously, the New Yorkers found something they like about him. However, they have failed to communicate that to the rest of the nation. As the Primary campaign continues, he will probably boost of his accomplishments.

But he doesn't stand out from the pack like Kamala Harris has done. You might not like her or her issues, but she is taking a stand and declaring her views with conviction.

My Prediction:

He drops out before Super Tuesday.

However, there is the possibility that he may be embraced by the far left and carried to the Democratic Party nomination. But the very forces that would carry him to the nomination would, in my opinion, make him unelectable in the General Election. As I've stated before and will undoubtedly mention several times in this book America is considered Center-Right. And that doesn't bode well for any Democratic candidate.

Mayor Bill de Blasio is in my opinion a joke. That's not politically correct and maybe not fair to say, but when you hear what he's been doing to the city of New York City, he's not very impressive. In fact, prior to the Primary I heard of him spoken of only in a negative fashion. He simply doesn't seem to have a real plan for the city and he certainly doesn't have one for the nation.

He will soon need to start telling the American people what he's all about. Not too long ago the American people voted for a man promising change and it can be said that he delivered. Unfortunately, it was eight years of undesirable change. And they were told to get used to it.

Now we have a President who promised a return to greatness and he's delivering on that promise. He's made changes that have the overall effect of helping the average person. If de Blasio truly wants to be the President of the United States, he needs to tell the American people who he is and what kind of change he will bring. He has stated his issues as we've seen above, but it appears to be a change for the worse rather than the better.

What am I saying? Basically, the American people were burned by a politician who promised them a lot of things and they, the American people, paid for it heavily. It played a large role in their turning to Trump. Now de Blasio comes around and makes generalized statements without a coherent plan. And, so far, the American people, particularly the Democratic base, are rejecting him.

At best I consider him a distant Dark Horse. And if he somehow manages to become the Democratic Nominee, he will have a rude awakening in the General Election.

But I predict he'll not do what needs to be done and will withdraw his candidacy probably before Super Tuesday.

FIVE : BOOKER

Cory Booker

Summary of Facts
U.S. Senator New Jersey

Party: Democrat

Tenure: 2013 - Present

Term Ends:

Years in Position: 6

Compensation Base salary $ 174,000
Net worth (2018) $ 600,000 to 1,300,000
Last elected: 2013
Education : Stanford, Oxford, Yale
Campaign Website: https://corybooker.com/
Political Leanings: Democrat; Far Left
Name Recognition: Medium
RealClearPolitics Poll: 07

Biography

Booker was born April 27, 1969 in Washington, D.C., but raised in Harrington Park, New Jersey. He later attended Stanford University receiving a B.A. and Masters. He also went to the University of Oxford on a Rhodes Scholarship and then Yale Law School.

Before becoming a Senator from New Jersey, he won election to the Municipal Council of Newark in 1998 where he made a name for himself by staging a 10-day hunger strike over urban development issues. He followed that up with a defeat in the mayoral race in 2002 but won in 2006. It was during Booker's tenure as the Mayor of Newark that affordable housing doubled, and the budget was reduced from $180 million to $73 million.

In 2013 he won the U.S Senate special election and won reelection in 2014 as the first African American U.S. Senator from New Jersey. As Senator he is rated as the third most liberal Senator and is considered a social liberal.

Among the issues he supports are women's rights, affirmative action, same-sex marriage, and single-payer healthcare all of which put him on the far left. However, he has also voted for the Employment Non-Discrimination Act of 2013, tougher sanctions against Iran, and sponsored the Bipartisan Budget Act of 2014.

Career

Senator, N.J. 2013-Present
Mayor of Newark, N.J. 2006-2013
City Councilman 1998-2002
Urban Justice Center
Private practice

ISSUES

Abortion
- Pro-Choice
- Supports denying the Right to Life for the unborn
- Supports abortion up to just prior to birth
- Opposes fetal heartbeat laws

Climate Change
- Supports Green New Deal
- Supports rejoining Paris Climate Accord

Criminal Justice
- Opposes packing the Supreme Court
- Supports term limits for Supreme Court Justices
- Supports reducing sentences for non-violent drug offenses

Economy
- Supports expanding Earned Income Tax Credits

Education
- Supports debt-free college

Election Reform
- Supports abolishing Electoral College
- Supports universal voter registration
- Supports former felons regaining voting rights

Foreign Relations
- Supported the Iran deal
- Opposes 'shadow' war with Syria

Guns
- Supports stricter gun laws
- Supports Universal background checks
- Supports mandatory gun licenses to purchase firearms
- Supports increased regulation of firearm manufacturers

Healthcare
- Supports Medicare-for-All

Housing
- Supports affordable housing

Immigration
- Supports prohibiting ICE from partnering with state and local law enforcement
- Supports expanding DACA protections

Marijuana
- Supports legalizing marijuana
- Supports expunging criminal records

Reparations
- Supports Reparations

Social Media
- Supports regulating Facebook and other Social Media.

My Analysis

These positions are counter to historical Americanism. Do we have a problem with immorality leading to unwanted births? Of course, we do, but the solution is not killing babies, but in reigning in illicit sex. Do we have a problem with people killing other people? Of course, we do, but making people defenseless is not the answer. Is undocumented immigration a problem? Of course, it is, but it won't be solved by opening our borders so that hundreds of thousands can enter and overwhelm our system. ICE needs to be strengthened, not unarmed.

Do we have a problem with Social Media, such as Facebook, acting like the morality police? Of course, we do, but regulating Social Media is dangerous ground and the First Amendment must be considered.

It would be better if all news outlets would self-regulate. One of the great things about blogs is the fact that the very name indicates it is someone's opinion. Newspapers, TV, etc. mix opinion and fact so that the general public is confused. A little self-regulation would restore the media's reputation.

As for Booker, here is my thinking on him.

Like most of the candidates Cory Booker is a Far-Left politician, but he often appears out of control. During the hearings regarding now Supreme Court Justice Anthony Cavanaugh Senator Booker showed a mean and dishonest streak.

To the Democratic base this will probably not hurt his chances in the Primary. They were opposed to Cavanaugh and, truth be told, he wasn't as offensive as others. Still he hasn't really stood out, although his RealClearPolitics has been strong.

He seems more of a Dark Horse than a real contender. But he is aggressive and Far Left. I think that gives him upward momentum. The question is how much and for how long will such momentum last?

My Prediction:

At this writing Booker hasn't broken out of the pack yet, but he bears watching. He's amid the pack and hasn't surged yet but could as the race moves forward. He could surge if he makes a move soon. The question is can he and will he. However, while the election is over a year away, as is the Convention. That seems like a long time, but it will go by quickly.

If he manages to win the Primary and be nominated, I don't see him doing well in the General Election. My prediction is that unless he states his position better and more often, he'll drop out before Super Tuesday.

SIX : BULLOCK

Steve Bullock

Summary of Facts

Governor, Montana

Tenure: 2012 - Present

Term Ends:

Years in Position: 7

Compensation Base salary $
Net worth (2016) $ 1,600,000
Last elected November 8, 2012
Education : Claremont Mckenna College; Columbia Law School
Campaign Website: https://stevebullock.com/
Political Leanings: Democrat; Far Left
Name Recognition: Poor
RealClearPolitics Poll: N/R

Biography

Bullock was born April 11, 1966 in Missoula, Montana. He graduated from Claremont McKenna College and Columbia Law School. His career has spanned both private and government. In private practice he was an attorney for Steptoe & Johnson. He was also an adjunct professor at the George Washington University Law School. At one point he had his own private law practice.

His government service has included legal counsel to the Secretary of State of Montana, Executive Assistant Attorney General, acting Chief Deputy Attorney General, and Attorney General of Montana. In 2012 he won the Governorship of Montana and was re-elected in 2016.

Career
Governor since 2013
State Attorney General single term
Attorney in State Attorney General office
Attorney in Secretary of State office.

ISSUES

Abortion
- Pro-Choice

Climate Change
- Opposes Green New Deal
- Supports renewable energy
- Supports stronger fuel efficiency standards
- Supports following the IPCC's recommendations

Criminal Justice Reform
- Supports term limits for Supreme Court Justices
- Supports adding justices (packing)

Economy
- Supports minimum wage increase (?)

Education
- Supports debt-free education

Election Reform
- Opposes abolishing Electoral College

Guns
- Supports universal background checks
- Supports magazine size restrictions

Healthcare
- Supports Medicare-for-All

Immigration
- Supports Dreamers

My Analysis

Bullock is another Far-Left candidate who knows how to use appealing words but doesn't tell us what it will cost and its impact on Middle America. The problem is that when any of the candidates do let us glimpse what it would cost, it is alarming.

The ideas that he and the other candidates favor would plunge our country back into a recession or possibly worse. Bullock has failed, as have the others, to see the correlation between the actions of President Trump and our bullish economy. Blacks, Latinos, and all Americans are benefiting enormously with rising employment and record setting low unemployment!

When they give reasons for needing their ideas, they describe an America that is fast disappearing. The traditional way of handling issues has always been throwing money upon a problem and hoping that will handle it. But it is like throwing money into a roaring fire which simply devours the money.

The liberal idea of class warfare (poor vs rich, etc.) has worked to keep them in power for decades. But the average American of all ethnic backgrounds, ages, and education are far more adept at using modern technology to find the truth. And when we look at what socialism (which most of their ideas fall under) has done in other countries, we don't really have any desire to see it here in America.

Bulloch's name recognition outside of Montana appears to be a non-event. But his ideas do carry weight in large liberal states. And this might give them the popular vote. But in a Representative Democracy like America the smaller states have a say and these liberal ideas are not soothing to their ears, which means Bullock and other liberals will most likely run into a wall in Mid-America. He'll be in an uphill fight as was evident in qualifying for the first debate where a candidate must have a minimum 1 percent in at least three approved polling organizations.

My Prediction:

Bullock has moved from the back of the pack to a higher though still low position in the polls. His RealClearPolitics rating of N/R (August 16, 2019) gives him very little name recognition and maneuvering room.

That means he needs to be going forward with the Far-Left agenda and with more energy than he's given so far. If he does that, he has a chance. But a year's worth of time to make a significant move is not really very long in politics.

Unless he begins moving forward soon, I predict he'll be out before Super Tuesday.

SEVEN : BUTTIGIEG

Pete Buttigieg

Summary of Facts

Mayor, South Bend, Ind.

Party: Democrat

Tenure: 2012 to Present

Term Ends: 2020

Years in Position:

Compensation Base salary $ 104,000
Net worth (2019) $ Royalties from book *Shortest Way Home*
Last elected November 8, 2016
Education : Harvard University, Pembroke (Rhodes Scholar)
Campaign Website: https://peteforamerica.com/
Political Leanings: Democrat; Moderately Left
Name Recognition: Poor
RealClearPolitics Poll: 05

Biography

Buttigieg was born January 19, 1982. He is a former military officer and combat veteran (2014 in Afghanistan). His education includes Harvard University, and Pembroke College, Oxford on a Rhodes Scholarship. His military service includes serving as an intelligence officer in the United States Navy Reserve achieving the rank of lieutenant.

In 2011 he was elected the Mayor of South Bend, Indiana and is the current mayor. In 2015 he came out publicly as gay prior to his re-election.

Career

Mayor of South Bend, Indiana

ISSUES

Theme

The focus of Buttigieg's campaign is on policy issues which line up with what he accomplished as the Mayor of South Bend, Indiana. He believes that government should be connecting with the global economy.

Abortion

- Pro-Choice
- Supports abortion
- Supports repeal of Hyde Amendment

Climate Change

- Supports Paris Climate Accord
- Supports Green New Deal

Criminal Justice Reform

- Opposes solitary confinement
- Opposes racial disparities in sentencing
- Opposes the death penalty
- Supports elimination of private prison industry
- Supports reforming pre-trial detention and cash bail
- Supports reduction of mass incarceration

Economy

- Supports taxing the rich
- Supports minimum wage of $15/hr.
- Supports universal basic income

Education

- Supports debt-free public college
- Supports increase in Pell grants
- Supports more support for 'Historically Black Colleges and Universities and Minority-Serving Institutions'
- Supports expansion of the Public Service Loan Forgiveness Program

Election Reform

- Supports structural reform on the Supreme Court
- Support expanding justices to 15 (5 left, 5 right, and 5 by consensus of the 10)
- Supports abolishing the Electoral College
- Supports automatic voter registration
- Supports early voting
- Supports making Election Day a national holiday
- Supports restoring voting rights to former felons

Foreign Relations

- Supports repealing and replacing the 2001 Authorization for the use of Military Force (AUMF)
- Support for withholding money from Israel if it annexes the West Bank
- Lukewarm support for Israel

Guns

- Supports universal background checks
- Supports banning military-style assault weapons
- Supports national gun licensing system

Healthcare

- Opposes Medicare-for-All
- Supports having a public option

Immigration

- Supports DACA
- Supports comprehensive immigration reform

LGBT

- Supports LBGT
- Is gay himself

Marijuana

- Supports legalization of marijuana

National Service

- Supports new service called Climate Corps
- Supports service centered on mental health

Reparation

- Supports reparations
- Supports empowerment of black America

- Supports investing in historically black colleges and universities

My analysis

Buttigieg's career is almost non-existent although he could argue he has more experience than Obama had. However, while that may ring well with fellow Democrats it's questionable how it will sound in mid-America.

Another issue that has been a Democratic issue since the 2016 election is not one that he has thought out. The issue is the Electoral College which gives all states, including Indiana, a level playing field. Overturning the Electoral College would in effect nullify the votes of Indiana citizens (for more on the Electoral College see chapter thirty-two).

My Prediction:

Although his RealClearPolitics rating puts him high in the standings, it is hard for me to see him as a viable candidate. If his rating remains high after Super Tuesday, I see him dropping out sometime between then and the Convention.

EIGHT : CASTRO

Julian Castro

Summary of Facts

Formerly
Secretary Housing & Urban Development

Tenure: 2010-2014

Compensation Base salary $
Net worth (2017) $ 138,00 – 470,000
Last elected: 2010
Education: Stanford, Harvard
Campaign Website: https://www.julianforthefuture.com/
Political Leanings: Democrat; Far Left
Name Recognition: Poor
RealClearPolitics Poll: 10

Biography

Castro was born September 16, 1974. According to his biography he was the youngest member of President Obama's Cabinet where he served as the 16th United States Secretary of Housing and Urban Development from 2014 to 2017.

Career

Secretary of Housing and Urban Development

Mayor, San Antonio, Texas

Aside from the offices he held, he was also mentioned as a possible running mate for Hillary Clinton in 2016.

(The following campaign themes were published on Castro's campaign website)

ISSUES

Abortion
- Pro-Choice
- Supports Roe v. Wade

Climate Change
- Supports Paris Climate Accord
- Supports Green New Deal

Criminal Justice Reform
- Supports limiting use of deadly force
- Supports disarming police
- Supports combating racially discriminatory policing

Economy
- Supports taxing the rich
- Supports 60-70% marginal tax rate for people making more than $10 million

Education
- Supports tuition-free public college, community college, & vocational schools
- Supports government funded universal pre-K
- Supports helping relieve student debt including loan forgiveness

Election Reform
- Supports abolish Electoral College
- Supports a national popular vote
- Opposes packing (expanding) Supreme Court
- Supports giving some, but not all, felons right to vote

Foreign Relations
- No policy statements

Healthcare
- Supports Medicare-for-All

Housing
- Supports tax credit for low and middle-income renters
- Supports establishing National Housing stabilization Fund
- Supports affordable housing

Guns
- Supports 'unite against' gun lobby
- Supports banning ownership of guns (NYT)

Immigration
- Supports breaking up ICE
- Supports path to citizenship for DREAMers
- Supports Open borders

Marijuana
- Supports legalization

Reparations
- Supports reparations, but no plan

My Analysis

Castro bears watching as his policies are far to the left which is exactly where the Democratic Party has moved. He also seems to have a way of expressing his policies in terms that should please the Far-Left community.

He lacks experience which will make him vulnerable on the campaign trail. Moreover, some of his claims are dubious. One such claim is that "lessened homelessness among our nation's veterans," which is interesting considering the extent of homeless veterans in 2016 after eight years of neglect while Secretary of Housing and Urban Development. He seems vulnerable on this and other claims.

My Prediction:

Despite his lack of experience, he may be in the battle to the end. His RealClearPolitics rank possibly encourages him to push forward. It is possible that his campaign could be energized enough for him to be a contender. It's also possible that he might be going into the convention with enough votes to force more than one ballot. Which brings up another point: If he wins the primary, I believe he will lose the General Election probably by a wide margin.

However, all of that is predicated on his campaign becoming energized which I haven't seen. I predict that he'll drop out after Super Tuesday and before the Convention.

NINE : CLINTON

Hillary Clinton

Summary of Facts

Former
Secretary of State

Party: Democrat

Tenure : 2009 - 2014

Term ended : 2014

Years in position : 5

Compensation Base salary   n/a
Net worth (2012) Est. $18,000,000
Education: Wellesley College, Yale
Campaign Website: n/a
Political Leanings: Democrat; Moderately Left
Name Recognition: Great
RealClearPolitics Poll: N/R

Biography

By most standards Hillary Clinton has had a remarkable career. It has spanned from Arkansas to Washington D.C. to New York. Yet she has little to show for such a long career. Her admirers claim she has accomplished a lot, yet when the opportunity comes to highlight them, we mostly get ideas promoted rather than bills introduced and passed.

She will be remembered though because of the deaths of Ambassador Stevens and others while she was Secretary of State. If she'd moved quickly and forthrightly, she could have made it a transforming moment that would have propelled her to the Presidency.

Instead, she tried to coverup the episode. We'll probably never know whether she was acting under orders from the President or acting on her own, but it undercut her credibility. If she'd shown more courage and transparency like the fictional Secretary on the TV show Madam Secretary, she'd been extremely hard to beat.

Career
Formerly Secretary of State: 2009-2014
First Lady
Secretary of State 2009-2014
U.S. Senator, NY
First Lady of Arkansas

ISSUES

Not declared; no issues

My Analysis
Clinton was plagued by controversy her entire political career. And her lack of being able to sell her ideas to the general public has brought about critical defeats culminating in her disastrous 2016 campaign.

Practically guaranteed a victory over an inexperienced non-politician she managed to look unpresidential in the debates. Sort of reminded me of Nixon when he lost to Kennedy. He looked unsure and unprepared; whereas Clinton looked overconfident, dismissive, and arrogant.

As First Lady, she and her husband campaigned for their universal health plan. They went on a national campaign promoting it and I noticed at the time that the more they talked enthusiastically about it the more it slipped in the polls. It lost and eventually became part of the basis for ObamaCare.

When running for the Presidency she took what most people thought was a shoo-in and lost first to an upstart with relatively no political experience by the name of Obama and then a second time when she lost her "guaranteed" victory to a non-political candidate called Trump. In between these losses and a poor performance as Secretary of State she managed to win in New York as their Senator where she had a mediocre record or at least had no meaningful successes that she could point to during the 2016 election.

At the time of the writing of this book former First Lady and former Secretary of State Hillary Clinton has not filed to run for the Presidency. And it would be understandable if she doesn't. Still, I'm assuming she will.

Perhaps she's hoping that if no candidate wins the Convention it will turn to her. Sounds unlikely, but a possible strategy.

Hillary Clinton has a lot of baggage that I believe will be detrimental to another run at the Presidency. Publicly she still is in denial over her loss. Whether she's made any changes to her political organization is unknown at this time.

The revelations of her using government documents on her private server will continue to haunt her in any future campaigns. The fact the revelations were illegally obtained matter little at this point. Her actions were at least unethical and probably illegal, thus hurting her.

She will also always be vulnerable on her record as Secretary of State. The death of an Ambassador and others on her watch will not go away and should not go away. It speaks of her lack of good judgment. Moreover, it shows a propensity to cover-up her mistakes.

Once the poster girl of the left I think they've moved further left than where she is. That probably dooms any political run by her. But being in self-denial herself, she just might attempt it. And her name is strong enough to maybe even give her the lead early on. But the Democratic Party's move to the far left will eventually overthrow her candidacy.

My Prediction:

Clinton, baggage and all, remains an intriguing figure in United States politics. And it might be noted that she still has legions of followers. So, it is possible that the temptation to mount up another campaign could be very enticing.

Because of the analysis above I don't really expect her to run for any office, much less the Presidency. And if she does decide to do so, I haven't seen nor heard of her coming to grips with her failure in 2016. As far as I know she still believes in Russian Collusion.

The above is somewhat amusing because the facts that have been revealed so far strongly suggest it was the Clinton Campaign that created the false narrative of Russian Collusion.

The interesting side note is that if Russia tried to interfere in the election in 2016 as many say they did then she would be wiser to blame the Russians. But if she refuses to acknowledge her own shortcomings, I don't believe she can mount an effective campaign simply because she won't change. Remember I said that in the debates she came across as being overconfident, dismissive, and arrogant. If she doesn't believe she lost the election, why should she change?

Therefore, if she does run for office, I believe she will drop out shortly after Super Tuesday for the reasons given above. If she doesn't run, it might make for an interesting convention if no one gets enough votes to be nominated. But I don't really see her as being chosen at the Convention. Aside from her baggage she's already a twice defeated Presidential candidate. Would the Party want to test the waters a third time?

If she runs, she's out shortly after Super Tuesday. Lock it in.

TEN : DELANEY

John Delaney

Summary of Facts

U.S. Representative for Maryland

Tenure: 2013-2019

Years in Position: 6

Compensation Base salary $ 174,000
Net worth (2015) $ 232,000,000
Last elected 2013
Education : Columbia, Georgetown
Campaign Website: https://www.johndelaney.com/
Political Leanings: Democrat; Moderately Left
Name Recognition: Poor
RealClearPolitics Poll: N/R

Biography

Delaney is the son of Jack and Elaine Delaney. Of Irish descent he was born and raised in New Jersey. He professes to be a Catholic and gives credit to his faith for some of his beliefs. He attended Columbia University and graduated in 1985. He later graduated from Georgetown

University Law Center in 1988. After that he received an honorary Doctor of Laws degree from Washington College in 2015.

Career
Representative for Maryland's 6th Congressional District

ISSUES

He emphasizes globalization, automation, and technology. Also, cooperation and bipartisanship and has pledged to only work on bipartisan proposals in first 100 days as President.

Abortion
- Pro-Choice
- Supports funding of Planned Parenthood

Climate Change
- Supports $4 trillion climate change plan
- Supports ending fossil fuel subsidies
- Supports electric transportation
- Supports 'Climate Corps' as new national service

Criminal Justice Reform
- Supports ending for-profit prisons
- Supports ending mandatory minimum sentences

Economy
- Opposes wealth tax
- Supports raising capital gains tax (matching with normal income tax rate)

Education
- Supports discharging student loan debt through bankruptcy

Election
- Opposes abolition of Electoral College
- Opposes expanding (packing) Supreme Court
- Supports stopping gerrymandering
- Supports independent commission to draw congressional boundaries
- Supports automatic voter registration

- Supports Election Day a national holiday
- Supports restoring Voting Rights Act

Foreign Relations

- Supports Iran nuclear deal
- Supports President Trump's progress with North Korea
- Supports small military presence in Afghanistan

Guns

- Supports universal background checks
- Supports limiting availability of military-style assault rifles
- Supports a national red flag law

Healthcare

- No policy statements

Immigration

- Supports path to citizenship for undocumented immigrants
- Opposes Open border

Marijuana

- Supports legalizing marijuana

National Service

- Supports national service program for young people graduating from high school

Reparations

- Supports reparations
- Supports commission to study & develop reparation proposals

My Analysis

Delaney is an interesting candidate. When examining his proposals, a person finds he is not nearly as far left as his fellow candidates. Some of his ideas might provide starting places with Republicans. One such proposal is Election Day becoming a national holiday. Such an idea could possibly increase voting.

Another interesting thing about Delaney is his pledge to only work on bipartisan proposals. That would be an interesting and possibly refreshing action.

But we will never know.

My Prediction:
Delaney is far back in the pack (he hovers around 14) and I haven't seen any movement. While he does have time, it is rapidly diminishing.
He will probably drop out before Super Tuesday.

ELEVEN : GABBARD

Tulsi Gabbard

Summary of Facts

U.S. House Hawaii District 2

Tenure: 2013 - Present

Term ends: 2021

Years in position: 6

Compensation Base salary $ 174,000

Net worth (2015) $ 208,504
Last elected : November 6, 2018
Education : Bachelor's, Hawaii Pacific University
Campaign Website: Tulsi2020.com
Political Leanings: Democrat; Far Left
Name Recognition: Poor
RealClearPolitics Poll: 9

Biography

Gabbard was born on April 12, 1981 in Tutuila, American Samoa. The fourth of five children born to Mike and Carol Gabbard, she was two years old when the family moved to Hawaii. Her father currently is a member of the Hawaii Senate.

She comes from a multicultural and multireligious family. Her father is of both Samoan and European ancestry and is a practicing Catholic. Meanwhile, her mother is originally from Decatur, Indiana, is of German descent and a practicing Hindu. Gabbard herself is a Hindu having chosen that as her religion when a teenager.

Career

- **2013-Present** U.S. Representative from Hawaii's 2nd Congressional District
- **2003-Present**: Company Commander, Hawaii Army National Guard
- **2010-2012**: Honolulu City Council
- **2009**: Graduated from Hawaii Pacific University with a bachelor's degree
- **2006-2007**: Legislative aide to Senator Daniel Akaka
- **2002-2004**: Hawaii House of Representatives
- **2003 to Present**: Army National Guard

She has already made history as one of the first two female combat veterans. Further, her political career in Congress has historical significance as she was the first Hindu and the first female of Samoan ancestry to serve there.

During her political career she has been focused on and has served on committees dealing with Homeland Security, Foreign Affairs, and the Armed Services. In addition, she is a strong supporter of gay rights.

ISSUES

Abortion
- Pro-Choice
- Supports Planned Parenthood
- Supports NARAL

Climate Change
- Supports renewable energy
- Supports wind production tax credit
- Supports solar investment tax credit
- Supports eliminating federal subsidies for fossil fuel

Criminal Justice Reform
- No policy statements

Economy
- Supports tax credits for businesses that hire workers unemployed for more than six months
- Supports eliminate redundant and unnecessary bureaucracy and regulations
- Supports tax breaks for corporations that outsource jobs overseas
- Supports reducing payroll taxes for small businesses
- Supports legislation providing access and opportunity to capital for small business owners
- Supports Wall Street reform
- Supports reinstating the Glass-Steagall Act
- Supports breaking up big banks

Education
- No policy statements

Election Reform
- No policy statements

Environment
- No policy statements

Foreign Relations
- Supports ending war to overthrow Syrian government
- Introduced four things to defeat ISIS and other jihadist groups

Guns
- Supports gun control
- Supports federal ban on military-style assault weapons
- Supports ban on high capacity magazines
- Supports comprehensive pre-purchase background checks

Healthcare
- Supports protecting Medicare
- Supports affordable healthcare for all (Medicare-for-All ?)
- Supports protecting Social Security

Housing
- Supports affordable housing
- Supports reducing high cost of living

Immigration
- No policy statements

Internet
Supports an open internet that is available to all

LGBT
- Supports LGBT

Marijuana
- No policy statements

Reparations
- No policy statements

Veterans
- Supports taking care of our veterans

My Analysis

In doing research on this candidate I think there are certain positions she holds that may help her in the Primary. For example, she supports Universal Healthcare (which may mean Medicare-for-All) which resonates well with the Far Left. Moreover, she supports Abortion (code named Women's Rights). That certainly is supported by the Far Left. Her positions on LGBT and gun control won't hurt her either.

The problem is that these issues won't win her many friends in Mid-America. Another problem of her own creation is the inclusion of sexual orientation and sexual identity as though these terms are found in our Constitution. They are not. And, somehow, she will have to convince people living in the Bible Belt that they should be included in the Constitution. No problem in the Primary, but the General Election it could become a major issue.

She is another one who might win the Primary Election and be nominated. But the General Election would be a different story. Yes, she'd probably get California and New York thereby gaining a large popular vote. But most of those votes would be concentrated in large states (same as any Democratic candidate).

Later in the book I have a chapter devoted to the fact that the United States is not and never has been a democracy. From the beginning it has been a Representative Democracy. It strains one's credibility to hear an apparently intelligent person argue that popular vote is fairer than an electoral vote. History depicts for us that the Electoral College despite its flaws is much fairer than the popular vote. It allows even the smallest state to have an important role in our elections.

Our forefathers purposely chose Representative Democracy over Democracy because they realized that there would always be large states that would thereby dominate the political landscape. Popular vote sounds great, but it would destroy America!

It is on this slippery ground that the Far Left has built the campaigns of most of the candidates. I sincerely doubt that Gabbard or any other Far Left candidate would have a chance against President Trump.

My Prediction:

As I have been writing this book I've had to stop and rethink my predictions as the political landscape is constantly moving. In effect, my crystal ball had to be changed as she stepped out of the pack during the first debate. If she continues to step forward and articulate her position well, then she is in the mix.

I haven't heard much about her since then. She made a move from a RealClearPolitics rank of 13 up to 9, which is a solid jump. If she can continue climbing, she could become a real contender, which makes her a person to watch.

In my opinion Gabbard is a Dark Horse. With Biden and Sanders slipping, she has a chance to contend with Elizabeth Warren and Kamala Harris. It may be a small chance, but it is a chance.

However, assuming I'm correct she hasn't staked out a position on the issues ('No policy statements'), she needs to take a stand on them. To win the nomination she will need to express herself in a way that furthers her leftward credentials. She is already Far Left but the absence of clear policy statements on these issues could conceivably hurt her in any matchup against Warren, Harris, or other strong candidates.

She certainly bears watching. If she wins the nomination, she will go on to lose the General Election against President Trump. However, I can see her doing better against Trump than Warren or anyone else.

Gabbard has been guilty, along with most of the candidates, of overlooking average Americans. We are, as I've stated before, a Center-Right nation. But she occupies the Far Left. Though the Far Left may take over the Democratic Party she will be out of step with the rest of the United States. That puts her at a tremendous disadvantage.

Trump should easily defeat her.

However, based on current performance I predict that she drops out after Super Tuesday and before the Convention.

TWELVE : GILLIBRAND

Kirsten Gillibrand

Summary of Facts

Senator, New York

Tenure: 2010 - Present

Compensation Base salary $ 174,000
Net worth (2018) $ 498,000
Education : Dartmouth, Beijing Normal University, UCLA
Campaign Website:
Political Leanings: Democrat; Far Left
Name Recognition: Poor
RealClearPolitics Poll: N/R

Biography

Gillibrand was born Kirsten Elizabeth Rutnik on December 9, 1966 in Albany, New York. She is the daughter of Douglas and Polly Rutnik who divorced in the late 1980's. Both parents are attorneys. Her father is also an associate of former Senator Alfonse M. D'Amato, while her grandmother, Polly Noonan, was the founder of the Albany Democratic

Women's Club and city leader of the Democratic political machine in Albany. She has a multicultural heritage. This heritage includes Austria, English, German, Irish, and Scottish ancestry.

Career

Senator, New York (2010 – Present)

Representative, New York 20th District (2007 – 2009)

ISSUES

Abortion

- Pro-Choice
- Supports Roe v. Wade
- Supports repealing the Hyde Amendment
- Supports repealing the 'gag rule' (Prohibiting abortion providers who accept federal funding/insurance from talking to patients about abortions
- Supports expansion of birth control access
- Supports sex education
- Supports family planning funding (Title X)

Climate Change

- Supports Green New Deal

Criminal Justice Reform

- Supports expansion (packing) Supreme Court
- Supports expunging old prison records
- Supports reforming sentencing laws
- Supports changing federal rules for prisons
- Supports ending cash bail

Education

- Supports a year of public service awarded with student loan debt forgiveness

Election Reform

- Supports abolishing Electoral College
- Supports replacing with popular vote
- Supports restoring Voting Rights Act
- Supports automatic voter registration

- Supports expanding online registration and early voting
- Supports Election Day becoming national holiday
- Supports ending gerrymandering
- Supports ending voter roll purges

Foreign Relations

- Supports the consent of Congress through new Authorizations for the Use of Military Force

Healthcare

- Supports Medicare for All
- Claims health care is a right

Guns

- Supports universal background checks
- Supports banning of assault rifles

Immigration

- Opposes the Wall
- Opposes separation of families

LGBT

- Supports same-sex marriage

Marijuana

- Supports legalizing marijuana
- Supports expunging records of non-violent marijuana-related crimes
- Supports requiring insurance companies to cover medical marijuana

Reparations

- Wants to study the problem

My Analysis

Gillibrand once was a respected conservative but as her career grew, she progressively turned to the Left. This was especially true once she became a senator. A study of her career shows her stands on the various issues have changed. Once a conservative with high conservative ranking, she has moved to the Left, that is the Far Left! I don't think this is an issue, but she could come under attack.

Her positions on abortion, guns, immigration, and Medicare have moved her to the far left, thus moving her away from heartland America.

It is obvious to me that she came under somebody's influence. Either that or she felt her career was more likely to advance within the Democratic Party if she tilted left.

I'm not a mind reader. So, I tend to favor both theories. Admittedly that is a rather sarcastic observation, but for a person to change her views so quickly and travel so far (from conservative to far left), it is questionable to say the least.

My Prediction:

With poor name recognition and a poor RealClearPolitics ranking, it's hard to see her moving upward. And I haven't seen nor heard her name mentioned except in relation to the debates.

That's a difficult position to be in, but that seems to be the truth. Can she muster enough momentum to move up and battle the leaders? Nothing's impossible in this political arena. But she must do something bold and maybe radical to bring attention to herself.

To answer the question, I do believe she's got time to make a move. Part of her problem is that she's just about as far left as you can go, so that leaves out moving further to the left. I would say that she needs to come up with an idea that grabs the soul of the Democrats at least as much as Medicare-for-All did earlier. She already has come out in support of that, so she needs to come up with something else.

She must do more than just support somebody else's idea; she must create her own idea.

That is a major obstacle to overcome. But I don't see any other way unless she is such an effective speaker that she can sell her herself to the public overwhelmingly.

I consider all of that to be extremely unlikely, but not impossible. So, she does have a chance, just not a good one.

So, my prediction is that she will pull out of the race before Super Tuesday.

THIRTEEN : GORE

Al Gore

Summary of Facts

Formerly
Vice President

Democrat

Term: 1993-2001

Compensation Base salary $ n/a

Net worth (2019) $ 300,000,000
Last elected : 1993
Education : Harvard
Campaign Website: n/a
Political Leanings: Democrat; Moderately Left
Name Recognition: Great
RealClearPolitics Poll: N/R

Biography

Born Albert Arnold Gore, Jr. on March 31, 1948, in Washington, D.C. his father, Albert Gore, Sr., was a Democratic U.S. Representative from Tennessee and later a senator (1953-1971). His mother, Pauline LaFon Gore, was among first women to graduate from Vanderbilt Law School.

Gore graduated from Harvard in 1969 and enlisted in the Army although he was opposed to the Vietnam War. He did so because he felt it was his civic duty. In 1971 he served in Vietnam for seven months until his enlistment ended. Upon returning to the United States he made a mark as a journalist.

In 1999, he made the statement that "I took the initiative in creating the Internet." This statement was largely taken out of context to indicate he claimed he created the internet. The fact is he was one of the leading voices for the internet. This misquote is still heard today.

My Analysis

I am sure the former Vice President would like to be President of the United States, but he's unlikely to achieve such a position anytime soon. Unfortunately for him, his primary claim to fame is the movie *An Inconvenient Truth* (a speculative movie promoted as fact) which pushed him to the highest level within the Climate Change movement.

But his lifestyle seems to indicate he doesn't believe in climate change. While facts are in short supply and the amount of energy he uses is questioned, the fact is he uses more than the average American. This is a case where perception is more important than facts. And the perception is he doesn't practice what he preaches. Whatever the facts may be, the truth is that perception hurts his image.

He has had an important career and made contributions to America; however, he is more centric than far left. He carries too much baggage aside from the Climate Change disconnect. His ability to overcome such political baggage will determine how high he rises in the primary and in the current political environment.

Even if nominated, the country has moved further right in recent years and that would find even his brand of liberalism to far left.

My Prediction:

If he enters the race, he may have a chance, but I think it unlikely that he will enter which is why there's no issues listed for him. But if he does, he might last past the Super Tuesday primaries, but that's a tribute to his smarts and knowledge of politics not to his political stance.

Therefore, my prediction is that if he enters, he drops out after Super Tuesday.

FOURTEEN : GRAVEL

Mike Gravel

Summary of Facts

Formerly,
U.S. Senator, Alaska

Compensation Base salary $
Net worth (2012) est. $ 411,006
Education : Assumption College, American International College,
　　　Columbia
Campaign Website: https://www.mikegravel.org/
Political Leanings: Democrat; Moderately Left
Name Recognition: Poor
RealClearPolitics Poll: N/R

Biography

　　The son of Alphonse and Marie Gravel (French-Canadian immigrants), Mike was born May 13, 1930 in Springfield, Massachusetts as one of five children. Growing up, he was educated as a Catholic, eventually attending for one-year Assumption College, Worcester, Massachusetts. Then he transferred to American International College.

In 1951 he enlisted in the U.S. Army and attended counterintelligence school at Fort Holabird, Maryland. He went to Officer Candidate School at Fort Benning, Georgia where he graduated as second lieutenant in 1952, He served in the Army's Communications Intelligence Service, infiltrated the French communist rallies, and became a first lieutenant as a Special Agent in the Counterintelligence Corps. He was discharged in 1954.

He entered Columbia University School of General Studies in New York City. He studied economics and graduated in 1956. He worked various jobs, including working in the investment bond department at Bankers Trust. It was during this time he left the Catholic religion.

Career

U.S. Senator, Alaska (1969-1981)
State Representative, Alaskan House (1963-1966)

ISSUES

No issues listed.

Gravel says he is running because, "Our only aim is pushing the field left by appearing in the Democratic debates." According to his campaign he will eventually withdraw and endorse the most progressive candidate.

My Analysis

People don't usually follow someone who's not serious about contending. Gravel's aim to push the Democratic Party left is hardly necessary and not likely to create excitement about him. This was evident when qualifying for the first primary debate where the rules required a candidate to meet polling/grassroots fundraising to get a debate spot.

He failed the benchmark and failed the cut. This may account for his decision that he really wants the office.

Prediction

Whatever his goals, I expect him to drop out prior to Super Tuesday.

FIFTEEN : HARRIS

Kamala Harris

Summary of Facts

U.S. Senator, California

Term: 2017 - 2023

Compensation Base salary $ 174,000
Net worth (2018) $ 391,000
Last elected : November 6, 2018
Education : Howard University
Campaign Website: https://kamalaharris.org/
Political Leanings: Democrat; Moderately Left
Name Recognition: Excellent
RealClearPolitics Poll: 04

Biography

Harris was born October 20, 1964 in Oakland, California. Her father, Donald Harris is Jamaican while her mother, Shyamala, is a Tamil Indian and Hindu. Kamala identifies with her Indian and Black heritage and in 2019 she said, "I am black and I am proud of it." When she was a seven-year-old child her parents divorced with her mother getting custody.

When she was 12, her mother moved them to Montreal, Quebec.

In 1981, Kamala went to Howard University in Washington, D.C. where she majored in economics and political science. Afterward she moved to California and attended the University of California, Hastings College of the Law and earned her Juris Doctor (J.D.) in 1989. In 1990 she was admitted to the State Bar of California.

Harris held many positions as her career advanced, but she seems to have made her mark as District Attorney of San Francisco. In 2004 she became District Attorney. That same year she managed to anger the San Francisco Police Department. She refused to seek the death penalty for the death of Police Officer Isaac Espinoza who was shot and killed in the line of duty. Instead she convicted the killer of murder who was sentenced to life in prison.

Her felony conviction rate went from 52% to 67% within three years (2003-2006). She also achieved a dramatic 85% conviction rate for homicides, and convictions of drug dealers increased from 56% in 2003 to 74% in 2006. In 2010 she was elected Attorney General of California and was reelected in 2014.

Recently it has come to light that as San Francisco District Attorney she withheld evidence about a lab technician who was "intentionally sabotaging her work and stealing drugs." Although Harris claims she didn't know about the lab tech's actions the presiding judge said prosecutors "at the highest levels ..." knew. It is unknown how this pending scandal will play out.

ISSUES

Abortion
- Pro-Choice
- Supports preventing states from enacting laws without first clearing with Justice Department
- Supports repeal of Hyde Amendment

Climate Change
- Supports giving grants to coastal communities to prepare for sea-level rise
- Supports the Green New Deal

Criminal Justice Reform

- Opposes death penalty (formerly supported it)
- Supported pardoning people convicted of drug-related crimes
- Supports expanding (packing) the Supreme Court

Economy
- Supports 'Equal Pay Certification' to prove companies not giving preferential treatment regarding pay, promotions, & more

Education
- Supports College For All Act (eliminating tuition/fees for public colleges/universities for Americans earning less than $125,000/yr.
- Supports a limited student loan debt forgiveness program

Election Reform
- Supports abolition of the Electoral College
- Supports updating and reinvigorating the Voting Rights Act

Foreign Relations
Supports Israel

Guns
- Supports universal background checks
- Supports ban on assault weapons

Healthcare
- Supports "Medicare-for-All with public option

Housing
- Supports Homeowners Bill of Rights
- Supports debt reduction for homeowners
- Supports refundable tax credit for families making less than $100,000/yr.
- Supports $100 billion program to help Americans of color buy homes
- Supports reforming eviction and screening processes

Immigration
- Supports possible abolishment of ICE
- Supports DACA

Marijuana
- Supports federal legalization of marijuana

- Supports expunging marijuana convictions from people's records

Reparations
- Supports reparations

My Analysis

Senator Kamala Harris's name is recognizable due to her caustic and biased manner that may have turned moderate and independent voters against her. However, during the first debate in June she came out the big winner. But now the scandal regarding her withholding evidence hurt her chances. This has dropped her back in the standings. The implication is her success is due largely to her aggressive behavior both in the Senate and in the Primary debates leaving her susceptible to her history.

Her support for Medicare-for-All with a public option puts her in the Moderately Left column as does her support for Israel. Yet in many ways she is Far Left. Because she favors the public option and supports Israel, I have marked her Moderately Left. But that is still very much Left.

My Prediction:

I know you're getting tired of hearing this, but the serious polls and observers see her moving into the top echelons of the Primary race but losing in the General Election. In the July 8, 2019 RealClearPolitics poll she had moved up to 2nd place behind Biden who was already slipping down.

I see her and Elizabeth Warren fighting for the nomination right up to the last. At this writing I see Kamala winning. It could go to the convention, but the outcome will favor her, and in the end, she will compete against President Trump.

How will she fair against the President? She knows how to fight and will give it her all, but I see him using her own feistiness against her. When all is said and done, she is to the far left; too far left for the Independents she'd need to beat him! So, she loses to Donald Trump! ***Decisively!***

SIXTEEN : HICKENLOOPER

John Hickenlooper

Summary of Facts

former
Governor, Colorado

Dropped out August 15, 2019

Compensation Base salary $
Net worth (2007) $ 5,800,000
Education : Wesleyan University
Campaign Website: https://www.hickenlooper.com/
Political Leanings: Democrat; Moderately Left
Name Recognition: medium
RealClearPolitics Poll: N/R

Biography

Hickenlooper was born to John and Anne Hickenlooper in Narberth, Pennsylvania. When he was still a young child his father died leaving his now widowed mother to raise him. He graduated in 1970 from The Haverford School, an independent boys school. He then attended Wesleyan University where he received a B.A. in English (1974) and a master's degree in geology (1980). Having graduated he went to work for Buckhorn Petroleum

Hickenlooper began his business career by working for Buckhorn Petroleum in Colorado in the early 1980s. He was laid off in 1986 when the company was sold. But within two years he and five business partners opened the Wynkoop Brewing Company brewpub. It was one of the first brewpubs and it proved to be a successful venture. When he sold his stake to a group of managers and employees in 2007, he was paid $7 million.

Career

Governor, Colorado
Mayor, Denver, Colorado

ISSUES

Abortion

- Pro-Choice
- Supports Planned Parenthood

Climate Change

- Opposes Green New Deal
- Supports fracking
- Supports Innovative methane emissions
- Supports expanding jobs in energy

Criminal Justice reform

- Supports recreational marijuana
- Opposes death penalty

Education

- Supports scholarship fund for low-income, high achieving students
- Increased tax support for schools

Economy

- Supports higher minimum wage

Election Reform

- Supports 15 days of federal early voting
- Supports expanding automatic voter registration
- Supports Same-day registration
- Supports vote by mail

Foreign Relations
- Supports NATO
- Supports Free and Fair trade

Guns
- Supports Universal background checks
- Banning high capacity magazines

Healthcare
- Supports private insurance
- Opposes Medicare-for-All
- Supports Universal Health care

Immigration
- Supports DACA
- Supports illegal immigrants accessing Social Services
- Supports immigration reform & border security

LGBTQ
- Longtime supporter of LGBTQ

Taxes
- Opposes tax cuts
- Supports tax increases

Trade
- Opposes Tariffs on China
- Supports free trade

MY ANALYSIS

Hickenlooper is a relatively unknown politician. That doesn't stop him from winning the nomination or at least making a strong run. But it is a hurtle he will have to overcome for that to happen. His name recognition out west is probably high and provides him a degree of support. That should help him in the overall standings. So, he has a base to operate from.

His poor ranking in the RealClearPolitics polls is a major hurtle for him to overcome. Part of this is because he is an unknown name, but it is also because his issues match fairly-well with the other contenders. And that is a problem.

For Hickenlooper to have any chance to win the nomination he must find some way to stand out from the crowd. So far, that has not happened. But there is still time to accomplish that feat. If he does, he has a chance of moving up.

My Prediction:
My prediction is that he will drop out before Super Tuesday.

August 15, 2019, Hickenlooper announced ending of his campaign.

SEVENTEEN : INSLEE

Jay Inslee

Summary of Facts

Governor, Washington

Compensation Base salary $ 170,000 + 43,000 pension
Net worth (2012) $
Education : University of Washington, Willamette School of Law
Campaign Website: https://www.jayinslee.com/
Political Leanings: Democrat; Moderately Left
Name Recognition: Medium
RealClearPolitics Poll: N/R

Biography

Inslee is the son of Frank and Adele Inslee. He was born February 9, 1951 as a fifth-generation Washingtonian. Jay's family is of English and Welsh descent.

In 1969 he graduated from High School and was granted a student deferment from the draft. He went on to graduate from the University of Washington in 1973 and from Willamette University School of Law in 1976. He received his J.D. from Willamette.

He became politically active in 1985 while advocating for the construction of a new high school. That led to him later going to become a U.S. Representative for the state of Washington and then the governorship.

Career

Governor, State of Washington
U.S. Representative for State of Washington

ISSUES

Abortion
- Pro-Choice
- Supports Planned Parenthood

Climate Change
- Opposes the Green New Deal
- Has supported fracking
- Favors increased regulation of methane emissions
- Supports Clean energy

Criminal Justice
- Supports recreational marijuana
- Decriminalization of marijuana at federal level and States' rights
- Opposes death penalty

Economy
- Supports federal/private business partnerships
- Supports raising minimum wage
- Supports vocational training and apprenticeships

Education
- Supports a scholarship fund
- Supports increased taxes to fund schools

Election Reform
- Supports voting rights protection
- Supports mandating 15 days of early voting for federal elections
- Supports expanding automatic voter registration, same-day registration, and vote-by-mail.

Foreign Relations
- o Strengthen America/NATO relationship
- o Restore free and fair trade

Healthcare
- o Supports universal healthcare
- o Opposes Medicare-for-All
- o Supports healthcare exchanges
- o Supports Public Option (allowing buy-in of programs like Medicare at affordable price).

Guns
- o Supports background checks
- o Supports banning high-capacity magazines

Immigration
- o Supports DACA
- o Supports state's non-enforcement of federal law
- o Supports Immigration reform

LGBTQ
Supports LGBTQ

Taxes
- o Opposed tax cut
- o Supported modest tax increases

Trade
- o Supports free trade
- o Opposes tariffs

My Analysis

Inslee has a decent position in the RealClearPolitics polls. As with other candidates he needs to clearly state his positions if he is to stand out. His positions on issues don't really do that since they are like the rest of the pack.

He has some odd positions. He opposes the death penalty an obviously is ignorant of the purpose of the death penalty. It is not meant as a deterrent but rather as a penalty. As for a deterrent it deters convicted murderers from ever repeating their crime and has a 100%

effective rate. Further, life in prison without parole is not an answer either as 'without parole' is a joke.

Another problem that he shares with his opponents is the socialistic nature of many of their 'solutions'. Basically, it is mixing government and private industry. It is part of the reason we now have such a huge and sometimes unwieldly government.

These are examples of positions not well thought out.

My Prediction:

Unless Inslee can stake out ground for himself, he will not stand out. And if that is the case, he won't win the nomination. I see him dropping out prior to Super Tuesday.

EIGHTEEN : KLOBUCHAR

Amy Klobuchar

Summary of Facts

Senator, Minnesota

Tenure: 2007 - Present

Compensation Base salary $ 174,000
Net worth (2018) $ 836,000 – 1,900,000
Education : Yale University, University of Chicago Law School
Campaign Website: https://amyklobuchar.com/
Political Leanings: Democrat; Moderately Left
Name Recognition: Poor
RealClearPolitics Poll: 09

Biography

Klobuchar is the daughter of Jim and Rose Klobuchar and was born in Plymouth, Minnesota. Her parents divorced when she was a teenager in high school.

She attended and graduated from Yale University in 1982. While there she interned for then Vice President Walter Mondale. She wrote a 250-

page thesis that covered the building of the Hubert H. Humphrey Metro dome.

After graduating from Yale, she went to the University of Chicago Law School. During her time there she was an associate editor of the *University of Chicago Law Review*. Upon graduating in 1985 she received her Juris Doctor (J.D.) degree.

ISSUES

Abortion

- Pro-Choice
- Opposes Right to Life
- Supports Roe v Wade; would codify in law if decision overturned in Supreme Court
- Opposes fetal heartbeat laws

Climate Change

- Supports Green Deal
- Supports Obama-era climate policies
- Supports the Paris climate accord
- Supports the Clean Power Plan
- Supports Obama's fuel-efficiency standards for vehicles

Criminal Justice Reform

- Supports getting more liberal judges
- Supports creating federal clemency advisory board
- Supports appointing a White House post, outside the Department of Justice, to shape policies on criminal justice reform

Economy

- Strict on mergers and acquisitions
- Supports federal data privacy legislation
- Supports raising tax code to 25%
- Supports raising minimum wage to $15/hr.

Education

- Supports free community college
- Supports better refinancing options for student debt
- Supports expansion of Pell grants

Election Reform
- Supports abolishing the Electoral College
- Supports electing the president by popular vote
- Supports federal automatic voter registration at age 18

Healthcare
- Supports a public option
- Interested in opioid crisis
- Supports research and care for Alzheimer's patients
- Interested research caregiving
- Supports importation of drugs
- Supports access to mental health treatment
- Supports lowering costs of prescription drugs

Foreign Relations
- No policy statements

Guns
- Supports an assault weapons ban
- Supports universal background checks

Immigration
- Supports pathway to citizenship for most undocumented immigrants
- Supports increase in legal immigration
- Supports reform of ICE

Marijuana
- Supports legalization of Marijuana
- Supports STATES Act
- Supports States having the right to make own determination

Reparations
- Supports reparations but 'it doesn't have to be a direct pay for each person

My Analysis

With a high RealClearPolitics ranking Klobuchar is well-position to step out of the pack and make a serious run for the nomination. Like the other candidates, however, she needs to identify herself as unique rather than a copy of her opponents. Put another way, her issues need to be more than just a clone of everybody else.

If she can do this, then she might make a serious run at the nomination.

My Prediction:

Unless Klobuchar can charge forward, she can't win. So far, I haven't seen any real movement. So, I predict that while she might last past Super Tuesday, shortly afterward she will drop out.

NINETEEN : MESSAM

Wayne Messam

Summary of Facts

Mayor, Miramar, FL

Tenure: 2015 - Present

Compensation Base salary $ 43,000
Net worth (2012) $ 500,000+ home
Education : Florida State University
Campaign Website: n/a
Political Leanings: Democrat; Far Left
Name Recognition: Poor
RealClearPolitics Poll: N/R

Biography

Messam was born of Jamaican parents Hubert and Delsey Messam. The fourth of five children, he was the first born in the United States in South Bay, Florida. Growing up he was educated at Glades Central High School in Belle Glade, Florida.

Later he attended Florida State University where he got his bachelor's degree in Management Information Systems. He was also a wide receiver for the Seminoles and a member of the 1993 national championship team. But he soon became interested in politics and eventually became the mayor of Miramar, Florida. Now he is seeking to become President of the United States.

Career
    Mayor, Miramar, FL
    Miramar City Commission

ISSUES

Abortion
- Pro-Choice
- Supports few, if any, limitations

Climate Change
- Supports Paris Climate Accord
- Supports banning fracking

Criminal Justice Reform
- No Policy Statements

Economy
- Supports restoring higher tax rates
- Supports higher minimum wage

Education
- Supports affordable education
- Supports relief for student debt through debt cancelation
- Supports using repealed 2017 tax cut to pay for plan

Election Reform
- Supports abolition of Electoral College

Foreign Relations
- Supports using tariffs to crack down on certain countries

Guns
- Supports local gun regulations
- Opposes arming educators and teachers with guns
- Supports banning assault weapons

Healthcare
- Open to Medicare-for-All
- Supports negotiating for lower cost drugs

Immigration

- Supports comprehensive immigration reform
- Supports working with Mexico
- Supports providing pathway to citizenship for undocumented immigrants who are working and law-abiding
- Supports citizenship for Dreamers
- Repeal statute on illegal entry

LGBT

- No Policy Statements

Marijuana

- Supports letting States decide

Reparations

- No Policy Statements

My Analysis

Wayne failed to make the cut for the first primary. The debate rules required that to qualify a candidate had to meet polling or grassroots fundraising to get a debate spot. This benchmark was set at a minimum 1 percent in at least three approved polling organizations.

Such a failure suggests that Messam hasn't and likely won't overcome the name recognition obstacle. In addition to that you will notice that a few issues where he has failed to make any real policy statements. The combination of these problems cripples his campaign.

Which would also suggest that his inclusion in the Presidential sweepstakes may be extremely short.

My Prediction:

Americans, including those who are Democrats, have seen what putting an inexperienced man into the White House can do. It's a mixed bag as it brought in Obama who couldn't solve the recession to the satisfaction of the average American and Trump who has brought greater prosperity, employment, and security to our nation. Do you risk getting another Obama when you really want a Trump-like man or woman?

It's to be remembered that there isn't a single candidate that comes close to a likeness to Trump. There's no one who has the ideology, the commitment, the willingness to risk his or her career, and the sheer guts to do what he or she thinks is right. The fact is Donald Trump is one of a kind who came along at just the right moment.

So, that means choosing a candidate with limited experience is very risky. I think those candidates with greater experience will fight it out for the nomination.

I predict that Messam will drop out before Super Tuesday.

TWENTY : MOULTON

Seth Moulton

Summary of Facts

U.S. Representative, Massachusetts

Tenure: 2014 - Present

Compensation Base salary $ 174,000
Net worth (2015) $ 71,011 (25,027 – 377,000
Education : Harvard
Campaign Website: https://sethmoulton.com/
Political Leanings: Democrat; Moderately Left
Name Recognition: Poor
RealClearPolitics Poll: N/R

Biography

Moulton was born in Salem, Massachusetts on October 24, 1978 to Wilbur Thomas Moulton, Jr. and Lynn Alice. He grew up in Marblehead, MA and graduated from Phillips Academy in Andover, MA. In 2001, a few months before the 9/11 attacks, he joined the Marine Corps and attended Officer Candidate School. Upon graduation as second lieutenant, he was one of first Marine Corp's member's to enter Baghdad.

As a Democratic legislator he's been a critic of President Trump and has likened him to Hitler. Even so, he's got a reputation as a bipartisan legislator (34th during 114th U.S. Congress's term). (Based on frequency of member's bills attracting co-sponsors from the opposite party and each member's cosponsoring of bills by members of the opposite party.)

Career
U.S. Representative, Massachusetts

ISSUES

Abortion
- Pro-Choice
- Supports few, if any, limitations

Climate Change
- Supports nuclear energy
- Supports Green New Deal

Criminal Justice Reform
- Supports abolishment of Capital Punishment/Death Penalty

Economy
- Supports $15 minimum wage
- Supports paid family and medical leave

Education
- Supports expanding or fixing existing debt-relief programs

Election Reform
- Supports abolishing Electoral College

Foreign Policy
- Opposes deploying troops into Iran
- Believes his military experience prepares him for political landscape that is dependent upon foreign police
- Supports Cybersecurity

Guns
- Supports banning assault weapons

- Supports universal background checks

Healthcare
- Opposes Medicare-for-All
- Supports building on ACA

Immigration
- Supports citizenship for Dreamers
- Supports repealing statute on illegal entry
- Opposes the Wall

LGBT
- Supports same-sex marriage
- Supports abortion rights

Marijuana
- Has used marijuana
- Supports legalization

Transportation
- Supports commuter rail lines
- Supports added funding

My Analysis

Moulton's name recognition is very poor. Equally bad is his RealClearPolitics rating which is N/R at the writing of this book. Although there is plenty of time for him to overcome this issue, I haven't seen any movement in that direction.

Except for Medicare-for-All, Moulton appears to stand with the Far-Left Candidates. Medicare-for-All is a Far-Left Health Care issue. Not supporting it drops him into the Moderately Left group.

Seth missed the cut for the first primary debate. The debate rules required that to qualify a candidate had to meet polling or grassroots fundraising to get a debate spot. This benchmark was set at a minimum 1 percent in at least three approved polling organizations.

Such a failure suggests that Moulton hasn't been and likely won't overcome the name recognition obstacle to his candidacy. Which would also suggest that his inclusion in the Presidential sweepstakes may be extremely short.

My Prediction:

A lot depends upon his debate appearances if he makes future cuts. So far, he hasn't succeeded. That being the case I have him dropping out before Super Tuesday.

TWENTY-ONE : O'ROURKE

Beto O'Rourke

Summary of Facts

Former
U.S. Representative, Texas

Compensation Base salary $
Net worth (2018) $ 9,000,000
Education : Columbia University
Campaign Website: https://betoorourke.com/
Political Leanings: Democrat; Moderately Left
Name Recognition: Medium
RealClearPolitics Poll: 06

Biography

Robert O'Rourke, the son of Pat and Melissa O'Rourke, was born on September 26, 1972 in El Paso, Texas. He was nicknamed 'Beto', which is a common Spanish-Portuguese nickname for first names that end in '-berto'. He has Irish and Welsh heritage in addition to his American South heritage.

He has unusually damaging baggage from his teen years. He'd been a member of a computer hacker group stealing secrets and releasing tools to others that allowed them to also hack computers that ran Microsoft's

Windows. He also wrote poems, etc. highlighting sex and murder. He has publicly expressed regret for these activities.

In his battle for the 2018 Texas Senate seat he lost by less than 3%. He proved to be a successful fundraiser by raising more than $38 million in the third quarter. This was about three times what Cruz raised. The $80 million he raised for the year was the highest of any candidate ever.

Although there'd been speculation throughout the campaign that he might run for President, which he denied, he and his wife decided after the election not to rule out a run.

ISSUES

Abortion
- Pro-Choice
- Supports few, if any, limitations

Climate Change
- Supports Green New Deal
- Supports paying farmers for climate friendly practices

Criminal Justice Reform
- Opposes death penalty
- Supports ending cash bail
- Supports ending mandatory minimum Sentencing

Economy
- Supports federal minimum wage to $15/hr.
- Supports raising taxes on corporations
- Supports boosting taxes on wealthy
- Supports regulating technology companies

Education
- Supports universal pre-kindergarten
- Supports expanding or fixing existing debt-relief programs
- Supports boosting teacher pay
- Supports paid family and medical leave

Election Reform
- Supports mandating paper ballots
- Supports abolishing Electoral College
- Supports felons in prison voting

Foreign Relations
- Supports boosting defense budget
- Supports bringing the troops home
- Supports stopping China's predatory policies; change approach
- Supports demanding changes to USMCA treaty
- Opposes using tariffs to pressure countries

Guns
- Supports voluntary buyback
- Supports universal background checks
- Supports gun licensing

Healthcare
- Supports rethinking ACA
- Supports public option
- Opposes Medicare-for-All
- Supports negotiating drug prices for Medicare outpatient prescription drugs

Immigration
- Supports citizenship for Dreamers
- Leave statute in place regarding illegal entry
- Supports tearing down parts of Wall

LGBT
- Supports same-sex marriage
- Opposes ban on Transgenders in the military

Marijuana
- Supports legalizing marijuana

Transportation
- Supports paying for infrastructure through changing taxes on corporations and the wealthy

Reparations
- Supports reparations

My Analysis

Aside from the teenage baggage which shouldn't be lightly dismissed, his issues place him so close to the far left that he shouldn't be ignored.

With these taken into consideration, he's in position to move upward. How he will fare against Harris and Warren is unknown. But his ability to raise funds is a major plus! His RealClearPolitics places him in the mix and positions him to make a move.

My Prediction:

Even with that analysis I find O'Rourke difficult to predict. Currently, I see three possible outcomes for him as the campaign continues.

The first is that he stays right where he is with no movement up or down. I doubt his fundraising can counterbalance lack of clarity on his stances. However, he has plenty of time to flesh out his policy issues and set himself up as a unique candidate that can successfully stand up to any of the top rung candidates.

The second is he moves into contention with both Harris and Warren. In this scenario it will come down to his debate performances against both Harris and Warren. That should be interesting.

The third possible outcome is he wins the nomination. I feel he's a dark horse, but he gave Ted Cruz, a strong Conservative and good debater, a tight race. So, if he demonstrates skill at raising money, proves to be an effective debater, spells out his policies clearly, and his opponents stumble, he has a chance.

What happens if he wins the nomination? Well, for one thing his confidence will go through the roof! He would go up against President Trump believing himself to be the superior debater.

But then reality would set in. Trump's record on both the domestic and international scenes have already been clearly shown (and felt!) by the average American voter. It's a record pure rhetoric cannot overcome. The Green New Deal will give voters a clear decision: back to the days of high unemployment and probable permanent loss of industries, or continue the jobs boom, a buyer's housing market, lowest unemployment in decades, and a strong presence internationally.

I just don't see Beto overcoming all of that plus his own baggage. My prediction is he loses the primary and drops out before the Convention.

TWENTY-TWO : RYAN

Tim Ryan

Summary of Facts

U.S. Representative, Ohio

Tenure: 2003 - Present

Compensation Base salary $ 174,000
Net worth (2017) $ 283,000
Education : Youngstown State Univ., Bowling Green State Univ., Franklin Pierce Law Center (JD)
Campaign Website:
Political Leanings: Democrat; Moderately Left
Name Recognition: Medium
RealClearPolitics Poll: N/R

Biography

The son of Allen and Rochelle Ryan, he was born in Niles, Ohio on July 16, 1973. His parents divorced when he was seven and he was raised by his mother.

After growing up and becoming a U.S. Representative, Ryan became active in several areas. One such area was the case of Adi Othman, an illegal immigrant. This man had lived in the United States for almost 40 years, was married with four children, and ran several businesses. Ryan took up his case.

In 2018 Othman was ordered deported, an act opposed by Ryan. As with most of the Left, he put family over the law and argued that Othman should stay. When the deportation took place, Ryan condemned it, saying, " watch these families get ripped apart is the most heartbreaking thing any American citizen could ever see …" To my knowledge Ryan has never addressed the fact that we are a law-abiding country and Othman was disobeying the law (i.e. committing a crime). Instead he focused strictly upon family, people of all political persuasions recognized as important.

CAREER
U.S. Representative (2003-Present)
Ohio State Senator (2000 – 2002)

ISSUES

Abortion
- Pro-Choice
- Supports few, if any, limitations

Agriculture
- Supports a new "family farm, 21st century style"

Climate Change
- Supports renewable energy
- Supports agriculture being used in climate action

Criminal Justice
- Reduce mandatory drug sentencing
- All police officers with bodycams
- Supports stopping Capital Punishment/Death Penalty for now

Economy
- Supports doubling union membership
- Supports increasing apprenticeships
- Supports minimum wage of $15
- Supports paid family and medical leave
- Supports tax increases
- Against tax cuts

Education
- Supports free college

- Supports expanding or fixing debt relief

Election Reform
- Supports mandating paper ballots
- Supports abolishing Electoral College

Foreign Relations
- Supported Obama's Iran nuclear deal
- Supports Israel's right to self-defense
- Supports boosting defense budget
- Supports keeping the troops deployed

Guns
- Supports voluntary gun buyback
- Supports universal background checks

Healthcare –
- Supports single-payer and Affordable Care Act
- Opposes Medicare-for-All
- Supports negotiating for Medicare, international reference pricing and promoting generics

Immigration
- Supports citizenship for Dreamers
- Supports leaving statute in place regarding illegal entry
- Opposes Wall funding

LGBT
- No Policy Statements

Marijuana
- Supports legalizing marijuana

Reparation
- Supports studying reparations

My Analysis

I gave him a Medium rating for name recognition. He gets most of that from his long career on the national scene. However, it could easily drop down to Poor simply because of his RealClearPolitics rating.

As with other candidates his issues are very similar and, therefore, his need to step out of the pack is his primary need right now. About the only areas that don't line up with the other candidates is his pro-Israeli stance and his opposition to Medicare-for-All.

Therefore, it's time for him to enunciate his positions with greater clarity and passion. It is not enough to simply parrot what everyone else is saying. He needs to have his own voice. Without that he can't expect to move upward in the polls, let alone compete for the nomination.

He needs to get more aggressive so that his RealClearPolitics rating rises to the top five. If he can do that then he has a chance, but he must act soon. It is true there is about a year before the Democratic Convention occurs, but that time frame will go past faster that it may appear.

Therefore, he needs to break out of the pack soon. But the problem for him is that everyone that's below 10 or even below 5 will be trying to break out of the pack. That makes his job harder.

My Prediction:

Ryan has shown passion for his causes while in the House, but he hasn't shown enough passion to move the needle during this election cycle. Unless he shows more passion and clarity, I don't see him contending for the nomination.

This is particularly important if he wishes to battle Harris passion for passion and Warren clarity for clarity. Failure in these contests would doom his candidacy. So far, I haven't seen any indication he will accomplish such a transformation.

That said, I don't count him out yet. There is a possibility that he will step forward and aggressively go after the prize. If he does that then he has a chance to win the nomination. So, he bears watching, but so far, he hasn't showed the necessary gumption to pull this off.

So, until I see him step out of the pack and go on attack, I will stick to my prediction that he drops out after Super Tuesday or maybe earlier.

TWENTY-THREE : SANDERS

Bernie Sanders

Summary of Facts

U.S. SENATOR, VERMONT

Independent

Term: 2007- Present

Compensation Base salary $ 174,000
Net worth (2017) $ 2,000,000+
Last elected : November 6, 2018
Education : Brooklyn College, University of Chicago
Campaign Website: https://berniesanders.com/
Political Leanings: Democrat; Far Left
Name Recognition: High
RealClearPolitics Poll: 03

Biography

Born September 8, 1941 in Brooklyn, New York it didn't take Sanders long to get involved in political activism. His brother Larry joined the Young Democrats of America and campaigned for Adlai Stevenson II in 1956 and Bernie got involved.

Thus, began his long political career.

In 1981 Sanders was elected as Mayor of Burlington, Vermont. Shortly afterward in 1984 he endorsed Walter Mondale as a Democratic presential candidate. The endorsement of Mondale was lukewarm at best and despite his comment suggesting Mondale would not be a great president.

But his endorsement of Jesse Jackson in 1988 was entirely different. His support was enthusiastic, and he was inspired by the Jackson campaign to work closer with the party.

It was during this and following years his views began being shaped. They've been called everything from New Dealer to Economic Socialism to Socialism. He's also been called a reformer of Capitalism. Probably Socialism fits him best although he doesn't believe in the government owning the means of production.

His political affiliations have also been more extensive than most politicians. They've ranged from the Liberty Union Party to the Socialist Workers Party to the Democratic Party to Independent. Although he now lists himself as an Independent, he is also a member of the Democratic Party and is running for the Democratic nomination.

Career

Senator, Vermont (2007-Present)
At-large Congressman, Vermont (1991-2007)
Mayor, Burlington, Vermont (1981-1989)

ISSUES

Abortion

- Pro-choice
- Opposes defunding Planned Parenthood

Climate Change

- Supports Green New Deal
- Supports banning Fracking
- Supports closing existing nuclear power reactors
- Supports investment (taxes) in infrastructure
- Opposes Dakota Access Pipeline

Criminal Justice Reform

- Opposes Capital Punishment/Death Penalty
- Opposes Cash Bail

- Opposes cocaine sentencing disparities
- Opposes mandatory minimum sentencing
- Opposes private prisons

Economy

- Supports raising minimum wage
- Supports trade unions
- Supports breaking up agribusiness
- Supports paying farmers to carry out climate-friendly practices
- Supports bringing back Glass-Steagall
- Supports raising taxes on the wealthy
- Supports paid family and medical leave

Education

- Supports universal free meals
- Supports tuition free college
- Supports canceling all student debt
- Supports raising teacher pay

Election Reform

- Mandate paper ballots
- Supports limiting spending
- Supports abolishing Electoral College
- Supports allowing felons to vote while in prison

Foreign Policy

- Opposes military spending
- Labor rights
- Environment
- Opposed new sanctions on Russia and Iran

Guns

- Supports banning assault weapons
- Supports universal federal background checks
- Supports closing gun show loophole

Healthcare

- Universal and single payer
- Supported Affordable Care Act

- Supports Medicare-for-All
- Paid Parental Leave
- Support negotiating for Medicare, international reference pricing, and promoting generics

Immigration

- Supported the DREAM Act
- Supports citizenship for Dreamers
- Supports repeal of statute regarding illegal entry
- Supported 2013 comprehensive immigration reform
- Opposes the Wall

LGBT

- Supports legalization of same-sex marriage

Marijuana

- Supports legalization

Reparations

- Supports studying Reparations

Social Security

- Supports expansion of Social Security

Taxes

- Favors progressive tax
- Remove cap on payroll tax on all incomes $250,000 and above

Trade

- Opposed NAFTA
- Opposed CAFTA
- Opposed PNTR
- Opposed Trans-Pacific Partnership

Transportation

- Supports boosting infrastructure spending

WAR

- Opposed invasion of Iraq
- Opposes Patriot Act
- Opposes intervention in Yemen

My Analysis

That is probably one of the most extensive Issues list. But the problem is that he doesn't spell out his ideas as clearly as does Warren. He is discovering that grand ideas aren't enough, you must understand how it is going to work and how it will be paid for.

Bernie is probably in it for the long haul. However, his campaign as mentioned above emphasizes ideas not actions. As one commentator has said he follows the European ideal of ideas not the American ideal of practical actions. His big idea is socialism (also called Democratic Socialism) and he fails to comprehend or resolve the issue that around the world socialism consistently fails. If it doesn't fail now, it will eventually fail.

Thus, I believe that in the end he will probably end up fourth place (behind Harris, Warren, and Biden) or lower with other candidates moving into the top tier. Unfortunately for him his day came and went. He can thank the Hillary Clinton campaign for using dirty politics to derail his previous candidacy and his opportunity to be president. Now he can only sit there and watch his 'students' pass him by.

With the Democratic Party moving further to the left, Bernie is no longer the 'Poster Child' of the party. Other candidates are now promoting the very ideas he first enumerated, but they are going a step further to come up with actual plans or programs to enact the same ideas he has promoted.

My Prediction:

It could be argued that Bernie Sanders lit the fires that are now consuming the Democratic Party. Back in 2016 the Democrats were just warming up to him, but things have changed since then. Now these same Democrats have a roaring fire under them. It's like the want to rush the demise of the party. Candidates are stumbling over each other and over themselves to see how outrageous their plans can be. There's no steady hand at the helm.

I don't know what he's thinking these days. Is he proud of his 'students' or concerned at their wild dash to extinction? You look at his Issues and he embraces just about every socialistic idea out there. Is that because he really believes in them or he's worried he's losing?

I suggest he not worry. He and Biden sort of represent the old guard and are being pushed aside. He's lit the fire and now that fire is roaring and will not stop until the Democratic Party is consumed.

It is my prediction that Bernie Sanders will probably be amid candidates right up to the end and possibly in the Democratic Convention. But he won't win.

CHAPTER TWENTY-FOUR : STEYER

Tom Stever

Summary of Facts

Philanthropist

Compensation Base salary $
Net worth (2019) $ 1,600,000,000+
Education : Stanford, Yale
Campaign Website: https://www.tomsteyer.com/about-tom/
Political Leanings: Democrat; Moderately Left
Name Recognition: Poor
RealClearPolitics Poll: N/R

Biography

Born on June 27, 1957, Tom Steyer grew up and became an American billionaire who is a philanthropist, environmentalist, and a liberal activist. He is the founder and former co-senior managing partner of Farallon Capital and the co-founder of Onecalifornia Bank (now Beneficial State Bank).

Steyer and his wife signed The Giving Pledge in 2010. This pledges them to donate half their fortune to charity during their lifetime. Selling his stake in Farallon in 2012, Steyer turned his attention to politics and the environment.

ISSUES

Abortion
- Probably Pro-Life
- Unclear on specifics

Climate Change
- Opposed Keystone Pipeline
- Supports renewable energy
- Joined Bill Gate's Breakthrough Energy Coalition
- Supports banning fracking

Criminal Justice Reform
- No Policy Statements

Economy
- Supports increasing taxes on wealthy Americas

Education
- No Policy Statements

Election Reform
- No Policy Statements

Foreign Relations
- No Policy Statements

Guns
- Support banning assault weapons
- Supports universal background checks

Healthcare
- Opposes Medicare-for-All
- Supports expanded coverage

Immigration
- Supports citizenship for DREAMERS
- Supports executive action to help them legalize now
- Supports repeal of statute on Illegal Entry
- Opposes funding the Wall

LGBT
- No Policy Statements

Marijuana
- No Policy Statements

Reparations

- No Policy Statements

My Analysis

Steyer was slow in putting out his policy statements and as you can readily tell he still has several "No Policy Statements" in the list of issues. However, he opposes Medicare-for-All and supports expanded coverage. That is an issue that separates the different candidates and marks him as Moderately Left.

It is somewhat disappointing that he hasn't done a good job at spelling out his stands, how they're funded, and how they would impact America. His being a philanthropist suggested to me that such details would have been common for him.

Another fact about Steyer is his total lack of government experience. Not only government but business experience as well. President Obama had no business experience, which showed up negatively in his decision making. On the other hand, President Trump had no previous political experience, but he picked up on the power tools quickly.

For Steyer, his lack of those experiences would make it very hard for him to operate as the President of the United States. Moreover, it takes charisma to downplay them and convince the electorate, including Republicans and Independents, that he's the man for the job.

I doubt he has the capacity to be a true leader, A philanthropist works with people to get the job done, but a government leader needs to be able to take command at critical junctures. Both Presidents Obama and Trump knew how to do that. They used different methods such as Obama relying on his Cabinet to get things done and Trump personally making sure things got done. It reflected their personal experiences and preferences.

This all works against Steyer which is a disaster for him. He has both poor name recognition and a low RealClearPolitics ranking. It doesn't look good for him.

My Prediction:

This looks like a man on a jaunt where he doesn't seriously consider himself as a candidate for office. If he truly wants to be elected, he needs to step forward very soon and start making a name for himself as the right man at the right time instead of being a cookie-cutter candidate.

I expect him to drop out prior to Super Tuesday.

TWENTY-FIVE: SWALWELL

Eric Swalwell

Summary of Facts

U.S. Representative, California

Tenure: 2013 to Present

DROPPED OUT JULY 8, 2019

Compensation Base salary $ 174,000
Net worth (2012) $
Education : Bachelor's, Hawaii Pacific University
Campaign Website:
Political Leanings: Democrat; Moderately Left
Name Recognition: Poor
RealClearPolitics Poll: N/R

Biography

Eric Swalwell was raised in Sac City, Iowa, and Dublin, California. While attending the University of Maryland, College Park, he served as a student liaison to the city council for College Park, Maryland. He then interned for Ellen Tauscher and worked as a deputy district attorney in Alameda County, California. Before being elected to the U.S. House, he served as a local appointee on Dublin commissions, and served one term elected to the Dublin City Council.

He was elected to the U.S. House in November 2012, defeating incumbent Pete Stark, a 40-year incumbent who had held the office since 1973. Stark was a fellow Democrat almost a half-century Swalwell's senior; Swalwell was born shortly after Stark's re-election to his fifth term in Congress in the 1980 election. Swalwell took office on January 3, 2013 and has held it ever since.

Issues

Abortion

- Pro-choice
- Supports repeal of Hyde Amendment

Climate Change

- Supports renewable energy
- Supports more regulation of fracking
- Ban offshore drilling

Criminal Justice

- Supports preventing Justice Department from interfering in commercial marijuana when legal in a state

Economy

- Supports $15 minimum wage
- Supports training and development of federal workers
- Supports increasing job opportunities in technology
- Supports increasing economic mobility for low and middle-class Americans
- Co-sponsored legislation allowing new small businesses in economically underdeveloped areas to put off paying payroll taxes for their first year of operation.
- Voted against fast track trade authority on jobs and the economy
- Voted against fast track trade authority on technology

Education

- Supports-interest free federal student loans
- Supports loan-free public college for students who do work-study and/or go into public service

Election Reform
- Supports increased regulation of campaign finance
- Supports increased public funding of elections
- Supports strengthening Voting Rights Act

Foreign Relations
- Supports bolstering human rights around the world
- Fighting terrorism
- Two state resolution of Israel/Palestine conflict

Guns
- Supports universal background checks
- Supports banning sales of assault weapons
- Federal buyback program

Healthcare
- Supports Medicare-for-All with public option
- Supports increased funding for research for ALS, cancer, etc.

Immigration
- Supports comprehensive reform
- Co-sponsored the DREAM Act of 2017
- Opposes the Wall
- Opposes ban on immigrants from certain Muslim nations

LGBTQ
- Co-sponsored the Equality Act (extending rights to LGBTQ)
- Supports equal rights for LGBT service members and veterans

My Assessment

Swalwell is well back in the pack and doesn't look like a winner at all. With the Far Left surging he's at a disadvantage just like the other moderates, even though they are doing better than he is doing.

Poor name recognition and RealClearPolitics ranking are hurting him. But his moderation regarding Medicare-for-All is what hurts him the most.

My Prediction:
Originally, I predicted that he'd drop out before Super Tuesday **but on July 8, 2019 he dropped out of the race**. He is the first casualty.

TWENTY-SIX: WARREN

Elizabeth Warren

Summary of Facts

Senator, Massachusetts

Tenure: 2013 - Present

Term: 2013 - Present

Compensation Base salary $ 174,000
Net worth (2017) $ 4,600,000 + 10,600,000 (combines w/husband)
Last elected : November 6, 2018
Education : University of Houston, Rutgers
Campaign Website: https://elizabethwarren.com/
Political Leanings: Democrat; Far Left
Name Recognition: High
RealClearPolitics Poll: 02

Biography

Born Elizabeth Ann Herring on June 22, 1949, Warren created a bit of a dust bowl with claims identifying herself as a minority in a directory of legal professors. In it she claimed she was of Cherokee and Delaware Indian heritage. She continued claiming this in 2016 and Trump called her on it. It was during this time that he dubbed her Pocahontas, a name that has stuck.

After the election, Senator Warren released a DNA test that she *likely* had a Native American ancestor six to 10 generations ago. Cherokee Nation Secretary of State Chuck Hoskin Jr. criticized the announcement, 'Senator Warren is undermining tribal interests with her continued claims of tribal heritage'.

It's been reported that Senator Warren has apologized to Cherokee Nation on January 31, 2019. She has also gone further and included a statement on her website saying the following, 'While these results shed additional light on Elizabeth Warren's family history, she has stated that she is not enrolled in a tribe and respects the distinction between ancestry and tribal citizenship, which is determined by tribes-and only tribes'.

Whether this settles the issue or not may depend on whether she wins the nomination. If she does, I can see 'Pocahontas' reappearing in the following General Election.

Career

Senator, Massachusetts

ISSUES

Abortion
- Pro-Choice
- Supports few, if any, limits

Climate Change
- Supports Green New Deal
- Supports banning Fracking
- Supports paying farmers to carry out climate friendly practices

Criminal Justice reform
- Supports abolishing Capital Punishment/Death Penalty
- Opposes Cash Bail
- Opposes mandatory minimum sentences
- Opposes private prisons

Economy
- Supports increasing taxes to pay for infrastructure
- Supports raising minimum wage to $15/hr.
- Supports affordable housing

- Supports bringing back Glass-Steagall
- Supports raising taxes on wealthy
- Supports new social programs
- Supports paid family and medical leave
- Supports breaking up Agribusiness

Education
- Supports free College
- Supports canceling some student debt

Election Reform
- Supports mandating paper ballots
- Supports limiting spending
- Supports abolishing Electoral College
- Supports restoring voting rights after prison

Foreign Relations
- Opposed to USMCA (US-MEX-CAN) agreement
- Opposed to ICE
- Opposed to U.S. involvement in Yemen war
- Supports using tariffs to crack down on certain countries
- Supports bringing the troops home

Guns
- Supports banning assault weapons
- Supports universal background checks

Healthcare
- Supports Medicare-for-All
- Supports negotiating for drug prices, reference pricing and U.S. government generics

Immigration
- Supports DACA
- Supports repealing statute regarding illegal entry
- Opposes the Wall

LGBT
- Supports LGBT
- Supports same-sex marriage

Marijuana
- Supports legalizing Marijuana

Reparations
- Supports studying Reparations

My Analysis

Elizabeth Warren has been a force ever since the campaigning began. At one point she was trailing Sanders and Biden, but then she began moving up. At the time of the writing of this book she was in second place behind Biden, who was slipping.

It must be remembered that this analysis and prediction concerns only the Democratic Primary, not the General Election. So, it is a race to see who is the most left-leaning candidate that the Democratic Party can present to the American public.

My Prediction:

Assuming Warren continues her upward climb, it is entirely possible she could win the Primary. I was predicting Kamal Harris to win the nomination, but Warren can't be overlooked and in fact with momentum on her side she looks like a winner right now.

Assuming she wins and is anointed at the Convention she will then not only face Donald Trump but her own history. I fully expect that 'Pocahontas' will again become a popular image of the senator.

Furthermore, her ideas and programs will come under serious review. Not by the Press, but by ordinary citizens who will reject her programs in part or entirely. Not only for their costs but also for the impractical and economic disasters associated with them.

This would place her outside the center of the American political experience which has moved to the right. She will have her fifteen minutes of fame, but at the end of the day she will lose to President Trump probably in a landslide!

TWENTY-SEVEN : WELD

Bill Weld

Summary of Facts

Former
Governor, Massachusetts

Republican

Term: 1991-1997

Compensation Base salary $
Education : Harvard, University College (Oxford), Harvard Law
Campaign Website: https://www.weld2020.org/
Political Leanings: Republican;
Name Recognition: Poor
RealClearPolitics Poll: N/R

Biography

Weld was born on July 1945 in Smithtown, New York to David and Mary Weld. David was an investment banker, while Mary was a descendant of William Floyd, a signer of the U.S. Declaration of Independence.

Weld attended Middlesex School in Concord, Massachusetts and went on to graduate from Harvard College in 1966 and later graduated from Harvard Law School in 1970.

Career

Governor, Massachusetts (1990 – 1997)

U.S. Assistant Attorney General for Criminal Division
U.S. Attorney for the District of Massachusetts

ISSUES

Abortion
- Pro-Choice

Climate Change
- Supports Paris Climate Accord

Criminal Justice Reform
- No Policy Statements

Economy
- Supports reducing military spending
- Supports balancing the budget
- Supports withdrawing forces from foreign engagements
- Supports refocusing American politics on domestic issues
- Supports cutting spending
- Supports cutting taxes

Education
- Supports charter schools

Election Reform
- No Policy Statements

Foreign Relations
- No Policy Statements

Guns
- No Policy Statements

Healthcare
- No Policy Statements

Immigration
- No Policy Statements

LGBT
- Supports same-sex marriage
- Believes same-sex marriage is a fundamental human right.

Marijuana
- Supports legalization of Marijuana (sits on board of directors of a cannabis company

- Supports rolling back federal regulations

Reparations

- No Policy Statements

My Analysis

Bill Weld ran for Vice President as a Libertarian in 2016. Having rejoined the Republican Party, he'd left it for the Libertarian, he is now running for President in the Republican Party. It is quite a leap from Republican to Libertarian and back to Republican, but I have not discovered the reasoning behind the jumps.

Perhaps he's looking for a home that promotes his career. This raises questions, for example, why not run as the Libertarian candidate, which seems more agreeable to his political views?

As a Republican he virtually has no chance against Trump, but it would seem he'd have a better chance in the Libertarian Party. Whatever the thinking he is running in the Republican Party in direct opposition to President Trump.

Prior to his Vice-Presidential run, he was Governor of Massachusetts from 1991 to 1997. This indicates that his politics are generally left. All in all, he seems to be all over the political map.

It seems illogical to me that he'd run against Trump in the same party that Trump's running in. Yet there he is. The thought has occurred to me that he's running as a Republican not to win the nomination but to possibly embarrass the President. This would be something like a trojan horse, providing an avenue for the eventual Democratic candidate to harvest Republicans leaning left. But, in this day and age that we live, I find such a strategy dubious.

That said, his chances of successfully opposing President Trump seem chancy at best.

My Prediction:

While figuring out where he stands on the issues and within the Primary may be confusing to all of us, predicting the outcome of his candidacy is relatively easy. Even if he had a clear and definitive campaign, I expect the former governor's campaign to implode before we ever get to Super Tuesday.

In the end we may never know what his rationale has been, but he will have gained his 15 minutes of fame.

TWENTY-EIGHT : WILLIAMSON

Marianne Williamson

Summary of Facts

No Political Office

Compensation Base salary $
Net worth (2014) $ 957,000 – 4,500,000
Education : Pomona College
Campaign Website: https://marianne.com/
Political Leanings: Democrat; Far Left
Name Recognition: Poor
RealClearPolitics Poll: 12

Biography

Williamson was born on July 8, 1952 in Houston, Texas to Samuel and Sophie Williamson. Later she studied theater and philosophy at Pomona College.

A conservative Jew, she's been involved in Project Angel Food, which is a volunteer food delivery program. This program serves home-bound victims of HIV/AIDS and other life-threatening illnesses. She's also a co-founder of Peace Alliance, a nonprofit grassroots education and advocacy organization supporting peace-building projects.

While she has run for election before (California's 33rd congressional district in 2014), she has never held a political office before in city, state, or federal.

Career
None

ISSUES

Abortion
- Pro-Choice

Climate Change
- Supports Paris Climate Accord
- Supports Green New Deal

Criminal Justice Reform
- Opposes adding justices to Supreme Court
- Supports studying and promoting restorative justice programs
- Supports increasing the number of life-skills programs in prison

Economy
- Support repealing 2017 tax cut
- Supports eliminating cap on payroll taxes
- Supports eliminating carried interest
- Supports eliminating ETF loopholes
- Supports raising the Estate tax
- Supports taxing billionaires
- Supports raising minimum wage to $15/hr.

Education
- Supports universal pre-K
- Supports maternal and paternal leave
- Supports mental health for children
- Supports free College
- Supports cancelation of college loans

Election Reform
- Supports abolishing Electoral College
- Supports lowering voting age to 16Supports ending party gerrymandering

- Supports eliminating 'unfounded' voting restrictions
- Supports Election Day as a holiday

Foreign Relations

- Supports creation of a Department of Peace

Guns

- Supports universal background checks
- Supports mandatory waiting periods
- Supports banning bump stocks
- Supports banning high capacity magazines
- Supports requiring child safety locks on all guns
- Support red flag laws

Healthcare

- Supports Medicare-for-All
- Supports providing citizens with help from nutritionists, health coaches, therapists, and mental health.
- Supports ending subsidies for unhealthy foods

Immigration

- Supports path to citizenship for all law-abiding, productive immigrants
- Supports ending family separation
- Supports use of electronic surveillance for border security
- Supports more patrol agents
- Supports DACA

LGBT

- Supports LGBT

Marijuana

- Supports legalizing Marijuana
- Supports releasing non-violent offenders

Reparations

- Supports Reparations of $200 to $500 billion dollars
- Supports using Reparations to fund educational and economic projects

My Analysis

The first thing that you notice is that Williamson has no political office experience whatsoever. President Trump had no previous political office experience when he ran for office yet ended up defeating well-known opponents and winning the Presidency. While it's true she's not a Donald Trump, she is similar in lack of experience. But when you examine her background you find her education could hardly prepare her for running a campaign. Even harder to overcome is her lack of meaningful business and/or political experience.

She has poor name recognition and a RealClearPolitics ranking that's outside the top tier. That's three marks against her. Still, President Obama had poor name recognition and at the beginning would have had a poor ranking with RealClearPolitics. Yet he not only won the nomination but went on to win the Presidency!

So, there is history on her side. However, it appears she doesn't have the political sense of Obama nor the smarts of Trump. I wouldn't count her out. It can be done. But she needs to stand out from the pack, which requires finding an issue to build upon. But her stands are basically the same as her opponents. It's a long climb upward.

My Prediction:

It would be easy to write Williamson off because of my assessment. However, the last two presidents have shown, as indicated above, that those difficulties can be overcome. Can she pull it off?

We simply don't know enough about her except what she's shown in the Primary debates. We don't know how well she can handle adversity. Nor have we seen her step out on her own.

The truth is that Williamson is such an unknown factor that it is practically impossible to know how she will do. We'll have to watch and see what develops.

However, going by the current situation and what we know right now, I am looking for her to drop out either before Super Tuesday or shortly after.

TWENTY-NINE : YANG

Andrew Yang

Summary of Facts

No Political Office

CEO Venture for America

Compensation Base salary $ 285,000
Net worth (2016) $ Unknown
Education : Brown University, Columbia Law School (JD)
Campaign Website: https://www.yang2020.com/
Political Leanings: Democrat; Far Left
Name Recognition: Poor
RealClearPolitics Poll: 08

Biography

Yang was born January 13, 1975 in Schenectady, New York. His parents were immigrants from Taiwan who'd met in graduate school at the University of California, Berkeley. As for Andrew he early in life felt the sting of racial slurs and being bullied. It shaped his life.

But instead of letting these things put him down he went on to make something of himself. He has taken pride in relating to the underdog which led him into several ventures and has shaped his thinking. He is the founder of Venture America (VFA). He has worked in startups and early-stage growth companies and served President Obama as a 'Presidential Ambassador for Global Entrepreneurship'.

Career

No political office.

ISSUES

Abortion

- Pro-Choice
- Supports universal access
- Supports placing state abortion laws under oversight of board of doctors
- Supports universal access to contraception

Climate Change

- Supports regulating & taxing greenhouse gas emissions
- Supports investment in large-scale geo-engineering measures
- Supports Paris Climate Accord

Criminal Justice Reform

- Supports 18-year term limits for Supreme Court justices
- Supports every President having ability to appoint new judges in 1st and 3rd year by staggering justices terms
- Supports reducing jail time for use of opioids
- Supports being tougher on Wall Street crime

Economy

- Supports Human-Centered Capitalism (see Analysis)
- Supports universal basic income *
- Supports taxing capital gains
- Supports a 0.1% tax on financial transactions
- Supports a Department of Technology

Education

- Supports free college

Election Reform

- Opposes abolishing Electoral College

- Supports reducing 3rd party spoiler candidates by implementing ranked-choice voting
- Supports automatic voter registration
- Supports restoration of voting rights for past felons (not murderers)
- Supports lessening number of offenses that trigger loss of voting rights
- Supports Election Day as a national holiday

Foreign Relations

- Supports restraints and judgment in sending troops into harm's way

Guns

- Supports a tiered licensing program akin to MVD for autos vs. truck drivers
- Supports deeper background checks for those seeking to buy assault weapons
- Supports rigorous training for those buying assault weapons

Healthcare

- Supports Medicare-for-All
- Supports paid family leave

Immigration

- Supports creating a tier of long-term permanent residency
- Supports deporting undocumented immigrants who do not enroll in the long-term program
- Supports a path to citizenship for undocumented immigrants in the program

LGBTQ

- Supports legislation against discrimination based on sexual orientation and gender identity

Marijuana

- Supports legalizing Marijuana
- Supports removing Marijuana from Controlled Substances Act

Reparations

- Supports reducing wealth disparities
- Supports endowments for Historically Black Colleges and Universities
- No Policy Statement on Reparations

*Universal Basic Income is a Freedom Check drawn from a Value Added Tax that gives everyone $1000 per month. This is not in addition to social welfare programs but in place of them. Beneficiaries would have to choose between the current food stamps or disability checks and the $1000 monthly check

My Analysis

Although Yang has poor name recognition, he finds himself in the top ten in the Primary rankings according to RealClearPolitics. This might be in part due to some very interesting Issues.

Yang is doing what I think other candidates need to do. That is advocated for something outside the Left's box. One of the Issues he champions is Term Limits for Supreme Court justices. That strikes me as one that should be looked at closely and carefully. It is certainly interesting.

My Prediction:

Yang can move upward. How well he performs against the aggressive Kamala Harris and Elisabeth Warren might determine how good his chances are. He is certainly in the running.

Therefore, I predict he'll be in the running up to and possibly into the Convention. If he makes it that far he just might win.

He gets a few hours rest and then goes up against Donald Trump. Trump in a landslide.

THIRTY : TRUMP

Donald Trump

Summary of Facts

President of the United States

Republican

Tenure: 2017-2021

Years in Office: 3 Years

(I broke the alphabetical reporting because Donald Trump is the President and therefore stands alone. Let's look at his short political career.)

Compensation Base salary $
Net worth (2019) $ Est.
Last elected : November 8, 2016
Education :
Campaign Website:
Political Leanings: Republican; Populist; Conservative
Name Recognition: Extremely High
RealClearPolitics Poll: 01

Biography

Trump published a website called Promises Kept listing the accomplishments of his presidency, as of February 2019. The promises that he's kept are shown below with a mixture of website and my observations. As an aside I have been watching elections since the 1950's. I have never seen any president try to keep their promises as Trump has done. He's tried to keep all though frustrated by Congress and he's kept most in-spite of Congress.

Career

President of the United States (2017 – Present)

Issues

Abortion

- Pro-Life

Agriculture

- More flexibility to states on issuing food stamps
- More flexibility for state operations of Supplemental Nutrition Assistance Program (SNAP)
- Creation of the Interagency Task Force on Agriculture and Rural Prosperity

Climate Change

- Repealed the Clean Power Plan that dictated EPA's control of energy content and restricted State's rights and authority

Criminal Justice Reform

- No Policy Statements

Economy

- His campaign promises triggered companies changed plans in 2016
- Added nearly 3 million new jobs in first year
- Unemployment fell to 3.8 in first year
- Economic confidence rebounded to record highs
- Manufacturing jobs grew at tremendous pace averaging 20,000 per month in first year

Education

- Supports expansion of school choice
- In FY 2018 budget request school choice was priority for increased funding
- Called upon and supports Betsy Devos as Secretary of Education

- Dept. of Education has overseen ESSA to empower States with flexibility to educate students

Election Reform

- No Policy Statements

Foreign Relations

- Promoted fair and reciprocal trade
- Exited TPP
- Renegotiated NAFTA
- NAFTA now before Congress
- Secured bilateral deals with major trading partners

Government

- Eliminated 22 regulations for every new regulatory action (67 eliminated, 3 new)
- In FY 2017 saved $8.1 billion in lifetime net regulatory cost savings
- Reenergized agricultural, energy, and infrastructure
- Signed 15 Congressional Review Act resolutions into law (more than any other president)
- Ended Paris Climate Agreement
- Rolled back job killing power plan
- Ended war on coal

Guns

- May support working with Democrats for meaningful gun control

Healthcare

- Declared Nationwide Public Health emergency on opioid crises
- Expanded rules under Controlled Substances Ace
- Created a bipartisan opioid omission
- Department of Agriculture provided more than $1 billion in FY 2017 improving access to health care for 2.5 million people
- Declared a Nationwide Public Health Emergency
- Signed International Narcotics Trafficking Emergency Response By Detecting incoming Contraband With Technology (INTERDICT Act)
- In 2017, HHS announced $485 million in grants to states and territories to combat opioids

- In FY 2017, HHS invested nearly $900 million in opioid-specific funding
- Proposed changes to Medicaid to combat the opioid crisis
- Secretary of Labor agreed to expand access to Association Health Plans (AHPs) that potentially allows America employers to form groups across State lines
- Determined CSR payments to insurance companies are unlawful
- Repealed Obamacare's individual mandate

Immigration
- Supports the Wall
- Works with other countries to accept immigrants

Law
- Nominated Neil Gorsuch, who was confirmed, to United States Supreme Court
- Nominated over 75 Federal judges
- 28 judges have been confirmed, including 14 circuit judges
- Implementing a comprehensive plan to reorganize executive branch
- Department of Defense (DOD) is conducting a full audit of the Pentagon

LGBT
- No Policy Statement

Marijuana
- No Policy Statement

National Security and Defense
- Rebuilt military
- Crushed ISIS
- Confronted rogue nations
- Revived National Space Council
- Elevated U.S. Cyber Command into a major warfighting command
- Empowered Secretary of Defense and military commanders to make decisions, seize the initiative without micromanagement from Washington
- Directed State Department to send aid through USAID directly to Christians and other minorities facing genocide in the Middle East

- Pushed for coalition and attended Global Center for Combating Extremist Ideology (empowering Muslim-majority countries in fighting radicalization
- NATO allies and partners increased troop contribution to NATO's Resolute Support Mission in Afghanistan
- Actively denying Iran all paths to a nuclear weapon
- Ordered missile strikes against a Syrian airbase in response to chemical weapon attacks originating at the base
- Imposed new sanctions of the Maduro dictatorship in Venezuela
- Imposed sanctions against 16 Russian entities and indicted individuals
- Called out Russian government for malicious cyber activity
- Announce Russia Magnitsky Sanctions and Global Magnitsky Sanctions
- Imposed export controls against two Russian companies helping Russia develop missiles violating INF Treaty
- Established the Election Infrastructure Government and Sector Coordinating Councils to increase coordination and information sharing across all levels of government and with private sector providers of voting and registration systems
- Gave military 2.4% pay raise, the biggest since 2010

Reparations

- No Policy Statement

Taxes

- First major tax reform signed in 30 years.
- Federal revenues are increasing as the economy grows.
- Over 4.8 million workers received increased wages or bonuses.
- $1.5 trillion in tax cuts to individuals.
- American families received $3.2 trillion in gross tax cuts, doubled the child tax credit, and doubled standard deduction.
- Repealed Obamacare's burdensome individual mandate.
- Lowered the corporate tax rate from 35% to 21%

Trade

- Withdrew from the Trans-Pacific Partnership

- Improved KORUS (Korea and United States) trade agreement allowing more U.S. automobile exports to South Korea and increased U.S. pharmaceutical access
- America agriculture has gained access to new markets

Technology
- Infrastructure Initiative to help ensure Americans living in rural communities have access to the quality infrastructure they deserve

Veterans
- Signed the Veterans Accountability and Whistleblower Protection Act allowing senior officials in V.A. to fire failing employees and establish safeguards to protect whistleblowers
- Signed the Veterans Appeals Improvement and Modernization Act
- Signed the Harry W. Colmery Veterans Educational Assistance Act thereby funding the post-9/11 GI Bill

My Analysis:

When they look at the Democratic lineup some pundits compare it to the 2016 Republican lineup. However, there is one major problem there. In 2016 there was one man, a non-politician, who was bold, spoke his heart, identified with the people, and cared less for political speech. That was Trump!

Further the Democrats have no-one like that in their entire lineup. And there is very little separation from top to bottom on programs and policies. I suggest this kills that comparison at the very beginning.

President Donald Trump has proven to be a dynamic and effective President. With a hostile press and Congressional opposition that borders on childishness he has made amazing strides.

He began his Presidency by doing something that no President, Democrat or Republican, has done in my lifetime.

"What is it?" you ask.

I referred to it above. In every election period the candidates make promises to the voters to get their vote. These promises are made with the candidate knowing full well that he or she may not be able to keep them because they depend on Congress's approval. So, I along with millions of others assumed that Trump would be the same. Get elected and then walk back the promises.

Instead he sought and got men and women to head the various departments who were passionate about those department promises. He thankfully had a reasonable and cooperative Congress and was able to get the people he wanted. Some are still with him and some didn't stay, but the fact is he sought out people to carry out his promises.

Even with the "turmoil" that in my opinion has been evident in almost all newly elected President's first year, he was able to keep most of his promises and tried to keep all. That is simply amazing!

Critics often refer to the number of people leaving his administration as something we should be concerned about. I think the changes have been more due to the fact he is a hard man to work for. He demands a lot! I for one am not concerned. Their job is to carry out his wishes and if they don't do it, they're fired or forced to resign.

While the Press is no friend of the President and rarely reports on his accomplishments, the American people know about them. You've seen the list given previously.

That is why his popularity has risen. The facts got out (his Tweets and the Internet) and the people liked what they saw. Even if they don't like him personally, he's had a good record in their eyes. Both his personal and job ratings hover within the 40-50% rating without his formally announcing. Now that he is a candidate that rating will probably increase.

When you combine all of that with the Democrats committing mass suicide (turning further to the left) President Trump has positioned himself well.

The Non-Issue

I have seen on the Internet and possibly in the Media the question, "Why do Christians support such a man to be President of the United States?"

This question presupposes several things. So, I will list my reasons for supporting him.

The accusations abound saying that Donald Trump is not a Christian, men don't change their stripes, and that he is guilty of lying, etc.

First, it is dangerous to judge God, which is what these criticisms amount to. Even if Trump is guilty as charged, he is certainly far better than Lot was in the Old Testament. Yet the Bible mentions Lot's "righteous soul" which is a statement indicating Lot's salvation. There are many Christians that don't match up to the Bible in doctrine and practice but that doesn't mean they're not Christians. Further, Trump claims to be a Christian and it would be dangerous for me or anyone else to claim otherwise. It is between him and God. (I might add he chose a born-again believer as his Vice President and has removed many antichristian regulations.)

Secondly, the accusations against Trump are sometimes decades old and never mentioned until recently. Moreover, no proof is ever offered. It's hinted at but somehow never appears. It's classic #MeToo!

Third, how do you know Trump isn't a Christian? There are a lot of Christians out there that if I met them in Heaven I'd be surprised. But only that person and God knows if he's really a Christian. Moreover, with Christianity under attack the President has been a friend to Christianity, has restored prayer in the Capital, selected a known Christian as his Vice President, and has actively supported issues Christians support (such as moving our Embassy to Jerusalem and supporting Pro-life legislation).

Fourth, the statement that men never change is an outright lie. It is true that man in his own power cannot change himself but read your Bible. God changed the hearts of men and women throughout Earth's history. The Apostle Paul went about persecuting Christians and may have been responsible for their deaths, but God saved him, gave him a new name and a new heart. From the moment of his salvation he was a changed man!

Fifth, the charge of lying. This charge is largely a Press myth. They misquote him or take a quote out of context and when he says he didn't say it they point to their lie and call him a liar. Many of you have listened to a speech he's given and then heard the "bobble heads" explain it. And you were left scratching your head. Politicians exaggerate all the time but when this non-politician exaggerates, he's called a liar.

Sixth, I would prefer that all our presidents had been Christians, but many have not lived lives that exemplified Christian values yet some of them have proven to be good presidents anyhow. We've also had at least one president that claimed to be a Christian and even taught Sunday School. Yet that president may never be listed as a great or even good president (unless the left writes history).

Whether he is or isn't a Christian, Donald Trump has been a dynamic president who's turned our government back to a Constitutional Representative Republic and has gotten the government out of the way of Christianity. God put him in office, and he deserves our prayers and support!

Seven, when I vote for a man or woman to be president, I look at the issues and their solutions. In 2008 and 2012 I opposed Obama not because he was accused of being a Muslim nor had a suspect birth, but because he supported policies that endangered our republic. By the way, a person's color, sex, or religion are not what you should consider to be constitutional requirements for any political office.

The question referred to earlier is usually expressed by people who themselves are not professing Christians and are only looking to denigrate the President and Christianity itself. It is a non-issue.

My Prediction:

This is the easiest prediction to be made.

First, there is the primary. He has only one opponent (Weld) and has a large and strong support among the party faithful. With his record I fully expect him to win the Primary and be re-elected President of the United States.

Why?

Because in the end it is his performance and accomplishments while in office that Heartland U.S.A. considers to be important. You realize that California and New York will vote against Trump, but the power still resides with the people. Democrats dismiss the so-called "flyover Zone" (Heartland or that area lying between California and New York) states to their own detriment. If they really cared they would not be selling out to the Socialists.

Another reason is also quite apparent. The Democrats are bent on political suicide. There is not a single candidate, except maybe Biden who's only recently been moving further left, that could be considered anywhere near American values. At this writing, it appears that the Democratic Party is and will continue to be ruled by a small but vociferous Far Left contingent. If I was a lifelong Democrat I'd be weeping!

THIRTY-ONE : POLLS

Presidential Polls

Question: Should we trust polls?

I read an article recently that claimed polls are just as accurate today as they were 75 years ago. That may be true, but that doesn't mean they are accurate.

Whether they are accurate or not our society is strongly influenced by polls. Part of the problem is that polls supposedly represent what Americans believe about any given subject. I get into that below, but this has made us lazy. We Americans like to be in the majority and so often we check the polls to discover how we should vote.

This is true not only in politics, but what doctors and hospitals we prefer, foods we eat, clothes we buy, businesses we frequent, and so much more. It is unhealthy and bad for our nation. But it is particularly bad in the political arena.

Unfortunately, polls are based on a flawed belief, namely that everything has been essentially the same from the beginning. As applied to polls it would mean that if you live in the same community, work in the same industry, make the same money, and worship in the same faith then you will vote the same. While a tendency may be in that direction it ignores human nature, which is usually independent.

We Americans are a funny lot. We like to be considered independent thinkers, yet we seek conformity in many things. Moreover, we want to be liked and accepted, but when freed from the observances of others we often differ. In addition, people in the same family can differ on political opinions. Polls don't take that into consideration.

Another weakness of polls is the way questions are worded. Sometimes they use false comparisons giving the person being polled if/or questions and shaping the question according to the polls bias. It is not necessarily a true comparison, but it can be effective in swaying how people answer the questions and what they believe. Then the results are published in the media and the general public gets a biased view of the subject or the candidate in question. This occurs in all elections, including the 2016 election. The sheer magnitude of Trump's victory is highlighted when you consider this fact.

The only true poll is the election itself. I tend to regard all polls as educated guesses depending upon the pollster's bias. Some polls claim to be unbiased, but this is contrary to human nature. All humans have biases. To learn what a poll's bias is simply study the polls' results, wording of questions, and who pays for it. You'll figure it out.

However, you may have noticed that I've used RealClearPolitics throughout this book and that is a compilation of polls. I use them only as a reference point to project a candidate's relative position. So, polls are useful. Just beware of placing too much reliance on them.

THIRTY-TWO: REPRESENTATIVE DEMOCRACY

Representative Democracy

A Representative Democracy is where each citizen shares equally in political privilege and duty and with his right to do so are protected by free elections and other guarantees. They elect representatives to carry out their wishes.

Technically a representative is supposed to reflect the will of the people. Today, representatives gather power unto themselves and act according to their own whims. All too many seem overly concerned with making money and staying in office.

Therefore, we often hear about Term Limits, but it is doubtful we'll ever see Term Limits for Representatives and/or Senators. You're asking them to vote to limit their own ability to stay in office!

The primary difference between Representative Democracy and (Pure) Democracy is the election of representatives. In Democracy, often called Pure Democracy, the power to legislate rests with the people directly. Sounds good on paper and can work in villages, and maybe a little higher. But when you get to cities, states, and the federal government it doesn't work. The higher you go the more difficult and dangerous they become.

In a country where Pure Democracy exists, you have every bill being brought to the people. There would be arguments, riots, and possibly uprisings. Government would slow to a crawl if it moved at all. The ability to respond to crises whether humanitarian, economic, war, or anything would be virtually nonexistent.

A Representative Democracy, even with its obvious shortcomings, is more flexible and produces more legislation in a single year than going directly to the people can ever do. The representatives are held accountable by having to face the voters who put them in office in an election. While this system may need a tweak here and there it isn't broken and should be preserved. One such tweak could be term limits for both representatives and senators.

Our forefathers recognized this fact and established us as a Representative Democracy. One example of this type of government is the Electoral College. In the General Election we elect men and women who will vote for the President of our choice. The idea is that "Each state shall appoint, in such Manner as the Legislature thereof may direct, a Number of Electors, equal to the whole Number of Senators and Representatives to which the State may be entitled in the Congress: but no Senator or Representative, or Person holding an Office of Trust or Profit under the United States, shall be appointed an Elector." (Article II, Section 1, paragraph 2 of U.S. Constitution.)

It is fair to say the Electoral College needs some reformation. But to do so should be done cautiously. Many of those spewing hatred for the Electoral College want to see our presidents elected by popular vote which would cause the big states like California, New York and a few others to dominate. Our forefathers recognized this danger and created the college. So, if it is changed it should be done so with great caution and awareness.

THIRTY-THREE : CAPITALISM VS. SOCIALISM

Capitalism

When our forefathers established our country, they chose a capitalistic system.

Why?

Because it allows the most people no matter their position within society to participate and benefit from the economy. We older folk grew up knowing many of the stories of men and women inventing something that elevated them into successful people to be admired. I wonder if these stories are ever heard today. Perhaps they are heard in a Private School, Home School, or Christian School, but I have real concerns and doubts that such is the case in Public Schools.

Before continuing let's define *Public Schools*. These are schools supported by our taxes. They are regulated by the government and therefore what they teach is what the government wants taught. A more accurate name is government schools. This is one of the reasons for Private, Home, and Christian schools existing.

Today our public schools teach a revised history. Instead of heroic founders of our nation, we read of their faults (judged by today's standards). Instead of showing how people of wealth sacrificed their homes, their freedom, their families, and their health (including lives) all for the dream of freedom modern history examines their faults and weaknesses. Instead of showing that people on both sides of the Civil War loved God and were troubled by the moral questions the war raised, we read judgmental records. In some cases, the stories are so altered that the truth is buried.

The Capitalist System is an environment that has given us the auto industry, telephones, a renewed space industry, and so much more. No other system has provided so much flexibility and success. Nor have they opened opportunities for the common man (black, white, red, etc.) to succeed like capitalism! Yes, capitalism is flawed because we, that is all humans, are flawed.

Of course, there have been those unscrupulous men who've used the system to defraud citizens of their earnings. It is not a product of the system but of human nature which the Bible calls wicked. Such men and women belong in jail.

Capitalism is not perfect and needs restraints, but we need to be very cautious about any restraints we devise. You want to protect the people, but you also want everyone to be able to achieve success on their own merits. It is a delicate balance, but a necessary one.

Socialism

Socialism these days is promoted with glittering promises that everyone will benefit from such an economic system. But this flies in the face of history.

Sometimes socialists come up with a good idea, but historically in almost every case its success was tied to efforts and ideas coming from capitalists.

According to the dictionary Socialism is 'Public collective ownership or control of the basic means of production, distribution, and exchange, with the avowed aim of operating for use rather than for profit, and of assuring an equitable share of goods, services, and welfare benefits'.

Now we hear about Democratic Socialism and the claim it is different. And they do use different terms and may even support plans that are not traditionally socialistic.

But Socialism is in the end no matter what it is called still Socialism. A more simplistic rendering, but one I believe is accurate, is Socialism is government having total control of your lives even down to your medical care, your bank accounts, your investments, and what you can do with your own land. You might add, in the case of Democratic Socialism, that it starts out with benign promises that allow certain non-socialistic things like having private insurance, but it ends with the government being the big owner.

Socialism comes in many forms. In the Primary debates you will probably hear different ideas about what Socialism is or isn't. Just remember that Socialism under any other name is still Socialism and you eventually lose your right to private ownership and private insurance.

It's Just OK?

In July 2019 the NY Times ran an article claiming America is 'just OK'. This misleading article showed other countries ahead of us in lower poverty rates, better education, better health care, etc. But what's not reported is that they are able to achieve these successes because the United States provides for their ability to do so. It is our money and protective military shield that enables them to have a high standard.

The truth is America is the best, the greatest country on Earth. Prove it, you say. OK. What country is most desired as a place to live? America!

America is the standard by which all other countries are compared. People are willing to break the law to come here. How many want to go to Luxembourg, Sweden, or Norway? People want to immigrate to the United States, which means we are the greatest!

Which System to Choose?

It is true that Socialistic ideas have entered our laws throughout our history and to some degree succeeded. But history shows or at least implies that it takes a Capitalist to make the Socialist ideas work.

A classic example is Social Security. It sprang out of a Socialist's desire to provide a protected retirement for those of us 55 or older. Today the system is in danger because of Congress's penchant for 'borrowing money' from the Social Security funds to pay for bills passed in Congress. They then write an 'IOU' that most people regard as worthless! This book is not meant to discuss this issue in any deep degree, but the practice is abhorrent to any thoughtful American.

Social Security is primarily a forced savings account. Most people could probably do better on their own, but you are not allowed to do so. Some more conservative politicians think people should have the right to opt out and invest the money where they deem appropriate.

It's a Capitalist idea that could not only save Social Security but allow greater flexibility for those who opt out. In a Socialistic government such flexibility would not be allowed.

So, which one do you choose?

It comes down to your personal choice. Do you choose Socialism that has a long list of failure or Capitalism which has a long list of success? It's still your choice, choose wisely.

Wait, what do you mean?

Search your country's history. Not a single invention succeeded because of socialism. Capitalism enabled a Tom Edison to invent the light bulb, a farmer by the name of Ford to invent the auto, and hundreds of other inventions by the common folk. Socialism may have entered the picture to correct a perceived problem, but it was capitalism that gave people the opportunity to invent and market their products. And like I said above I believe that capitalism was needed to make the socialistic idea work.

How does this concern the election?

The President of the United States not only has great executive power but also has great influence. In 2020 the person who is elected President of the United States will be in position to influence legislation, especially if the same party controls Congress.

Virtually all Democratic candidates have signaled that they favor some form of socialism. On the Republican side stands Trump favoring capitalism. This suggests the importance of this election.

The man or woman you elect will bring his or her views into government and will by nature of the office have a lot to say about the future of America.

An interesting picture of this influence is the eight years of Obama's socialistic approach and the less than three years of Trump's capitalist approach. President Obama inherited the recession and is no more responsible for it than he is responsible for its end in 2010, a date set by number crunchers. The rest of us saw nothing changed until after Trump's election.

Although Obama and others have claimed the current economic expansion is a result of his policies, the truth is that business's reacted positively to the removal of his overbearing restrictions. This reaction led to business expansion and an explosion of hiring employees that began under Obama but were inspired by Trump's election and their confidence he'd keep his promises. This phenomenon is treated further in the chapter on the Economy.

The recession provides a stark contrast of the two systems!

THIRTY-FOUR : SEPARATION OF CHURCH AND STATE

History

The history of this issue began with a group of Baptist ministers who wrote a letter to President Thomas Jefferson. These men, who were concerned about freedom of religion were of the Committee of the Danbury Baptist Association in the State of Connecticut, wrote of these concerns to him. Here, in part, is their letter.

... Our sentiments are uniformly *on the side of religious liberty*: *that Religion is at all times and places a matter between God and individuals, that no man ought to suffer in name, person, or effects on account of his religious opinions,* [and] that *the legitimate power of civil government extends no further than to punish the man who works ill to his neighbor.* But sir, our constitution of government is not specific. Our ancient charter, together with the laws made coincident therewith, were adopted as the basis of our government at the time of our revolution. And such has been our laws and usages, and such still are, [so] *that Religion is considered as the first object of Legislation, and therefore what religious privileges we enjoy (as a minor part of the State) we enjoy as favors granted, and not as inalienable rights.* And these favors we receive at the expense of such degrading acknowledgments, as are *inconsistent with the rights of freemen.* It is not to be wondered at therefore, if *those who seek after power and gain, under the pretense of government and Religion, should reproach their fellow men,* [or] *should reproach their Chief Magistrate, as an enemy of religion, law, and good order, because he will not, dares not, assume the prerogative of Jehovah and make laws to govern the Kingdom of Christ.*

I've highlighted with italics portions for your better reading and understanding. Notice that they were concerned about the inalienable rights of religion. Further they were concerned with the government overreaching and 'make laws to govern the Kingdom of Christ'.

The President responded and I here include portions: ... Believing with you that *religion is a matter which lies solely between man and his God, that he owes account to none other for his faith or his worship, that the legislative powers of government reach actions only, and not opinions, I contemplate with sovereign reverence that act of the whole American people which declared that their legislature would "make no law respecting an establishment of religion, or prohibiting the free exercise thereof," thus building a wall of separation between Church and State.* Adhering to this expression of the supreme will of the nation *in behalf of the rights of conscience*, I shall see with sincere satisfaction the progress of those sentiments which tend to restore to man all his natural rights, convinced he has no natural right in opposition to his social duties.

I've highlighted with italics portions for your better understanding.

It is interesting to note that Jefferson borrowed the phrase, "wall of separation" from a Baptist and supporter of religious freedom.

Another important distinction is that the term "wall of separation" exists nowhere in the Constitution. This was a letter without any government power behind it. It was Jefferson's understanding, which by the way, agreed and replied to the Baptist's concerns.

It is unfortunate that the term "wall of separation" has been so twisted from its original meaning as to now mean government not being influenced by religion. Politicians and courts have ascribed this meaning to the term despite its clear history and wording. Even though these letters are not part of the Constitution.

At the time of the writing of these letters there were state governments that required church membership to be citizens of the state. In effect the church was under the control of the state. To be part of another denomination, such as Baptist, was considered illegal. Violation of these laws meant arrest, flogging, whippings, and other abuses. The whole issue was that religion (worship of God) was an inalienable right not a privilege to be given by the government! It is yours and my right!

It was the belief that everyone was answerable to God and their belief and that the worship of God was not subject to the rule of government. It means you could worship God as a Baptist, a Methodist, a Catholic, a Mormon, or any other religion. In fact, in my understanding you could choose not to worship God. You are answerable to ***God Alone***!

By the way, the modern phrase heard so often that Christians "shove their religion" down the throats of their fellow Americans has no proof or evidence supporting it. Instead, Christians fought and died along with others that all men might have the freedom to worship God as they believed was right.

It is true that we Christians are deeply concerned about the road our nation has been following for decades. We are not surprised that when God was kicked out of school the schools stopped teaching the Ten Commandments and children grew up with no moral compass. Today we are experiencing the spoiled fruit. You only need to pick up the paper or turn on the News to see that spoiled fruit in action.

What the critics contend are actions forcing Christianity down their throats is nothing more than Christians standing firm in their beliefs and not bowing to disbelievers who are literally shoving their beliefs down our throats. Look about you. In some communities Christians are persecuted while other beliefs are given a pass.

Take our public schools. It is allowed throughout the country for religious groups to use school facilities for their events. But when Christian groups want to use these same facilities they are refused or sued based on government having a 'wall of separation' between them and religion. Their only recourse is to sue the government so they can worship God freely.

Perhaps one of the most disturbing trends in our society is the turning of evil to good as we were warned in Romans:

"For the wrath of God is revealed from heaven against all ungodliness and unrighteousness of men, who hold the truth in unrighteousness; because that which may be known of God is manifest in them; for God hath shewed it unto them.

"For the invisible things of him from the creation of the world are clearly seen, being understood by the things that are made, even his eternal power and Godhead; so that they are without excuse: because that, when they knew God, they glorified him not as God, neither were thankful; but became vain in their imaginations, and their foolish heart was darkened.

"Professing themselves to be wise, they became fools."

Today the 'end justifies the means' is the mantra of the those claiming to be more moral. The LGBTQ+ crowd demands that the Bible not be used against them. They even try to change the Bible to show that they are the ones being persecuted. Nowadays they even are engaged in queering the Bible (an attempt to twist the Bible into supporting them). We live in a sad time.

THIRTY-FIVE : THE RIGHT TO VOTE

Your Vote Matters

"Your vote is your way of being represented in government. That means that when you vote you are making your needs and values known to the leaders of your country, state, and city. Your vote is your voice. If you do not use your vote, no one will hear you." (Ohio Literacy Network article at http://literacy.kent.edu/Oasis/Resc/Educ/vote1.html).

Is it a Right or Privilege?

The United States Constitution prohibits denial of the right to vote but doesn't expressly state it's a right. When the XV Amendment says, "Section 1. The **right** of citizens of the United States to **vote** shall not be denied or abridged by the United States or by any State on account of race, color, or previous condition of servitude" it certainly implies there is a right. If the 'right … to vote shall not be denied' then plain language says it's a right of every citizen! (Notice it doesn't say every person living in America, but every citizen!)

To the question about Right or Privilege I would answer both. Citizens have the right to vote when they reach a certain age, but it is a privilege that can be lost or taken away under certain circumstances (such as being in prison or not registering).

Qualifications

In the election of the President: **You can vote in United States elections if you:**

- Are a U.S. citizen.
- Meet your state's residency **requirements**. You can be a homeless person and still meet these r**equirements**.
- Are 18 years old on or before **Election** Day. ...
- Are registered to **vote** by your state's voter registration deadline.
  (usa.gov/right-to-vote)

So, while lawyers may argue about whether you have or don't have the right to vote, common sense tells us that it was assumed by the founders of our nation and by the authors of amendments that further delineated it.

So, let's summarize it this way: ***If you are a citizen of the United States of America <u>you have the right to vote</u>. But if you don't vote (by not registering or voting) you can lose the privilege. Moreover, if you are convicted of a crime you can lose the right to vote while in prison. Some states allow you to regain your vote after you leave prison.***

VOTE!

THIRTY-SIX : ARE FACT CHECKERS RELIABLE?

Fact Checkers

According to Wikipedia "**Fact-checking** is the act of checking factual assertions in non-fictional text in order to determine the veracity and correctness of the factual statements in the text."

For the purposes of this book we are concerned only with fact-checking after the publication (post-hoc fact-checking) of the "fact." In other words, it is checking up on statements and quotes to see if what was said either vocally or in print was accurate, inaccurate, or false.

I believe that fact checker's statements should be announced the same way polls are announced: *This fact check has a +- 5% chance of error*. At least we'd be warned.

The article I reviewed assumes that there are 'non-partisan neutral source' fact-checkers. That is a mouthful. What is being said is simply that the fact-checkers are unbiased.

It should be understood by all discerning voters that there simply isn't any such animal. All organizations are made up of human beings and all human beings are subject to bias of one form or another. It may be a good bias or a bad bias, but it is still a bias. For example, at the beginning of this book I stated that I'm a conservative. So, while I've sincerely tried to be fair and honest in my writing, I have a conservative bias. By the way, that's a good bias.

The idea of neutral presupposes no bias yet bias always exists. Don't believe me? Next time you check out a so-called neutral fact-checker, examine their record. You will find that most probably lean left, while there may be some leaning right. They may try to be neutral but if you look closely, you'll discover some bias.

So, are fact-checkers reliable? To answer that you simply need to ask yourself a few questions.

1. How do they pose their questions or quote the 'fact'?
2. Who pays their bill?
3. How strong is their bias?

If you have a clear understanding of the answers to these three questions, then you can discern how accurate they are. But overriding it all I suggest you follow this principle: *Never assume they are the final word on accuracy.*

For example, have you ever watched a political speech and then afterward heard the fact-checkers state certain remarks were false or wrong? I have. I have also heard them state afterward that certain statements were true or correct. Yet in their analysis they took the statements out of context and, in some cases, changed the wording. In this way they can deliver the news in a 'factual' manner that tends to support their primary view. Their bias provided the context of the remarks and the analysis of the remarks.

Admittedly these were reporters (not generally known for truthfulness). So, they get to pick and choose which fact-checkers they use. But my point is that this fact-checking of politicians is often at odds with what the viewer just saw and heard.

In my opinion, if you have doubts about certain facts a politician says, *do your **own** research*. If you're serious, you can start by getting the printed version of the speech. Then you'll have the complete speech to compare with the 'expert's' opinion. Yes, you will be approaching the subject with your own bias, but at least you can bring the truth to light. In this world of computers and Internet there is nothing stopping you!

Today we live in a world where reporters and fact-checkers feel they are empowered to have an impact on society and if they must smudge the facts a little, so be it. As a result, you and I must be more diligent than ever.

What about the Internet?

The internet involves a lot of high tech but in the end, it is still human beings entering data that you eventually access. How they do things may be different and it certainly seems easier to control. But you're still dealing with humans and that means you must be alert. Just like TV, Radio, and Newspapers you need to exercise discernment and not take things for granted. After a while you will learn what sources you can trust or mistrust.

You can choose whom to believe, but again your own biases will influence your choices. To be informed, get to the truth - listen to the actual statements *in context*.

In our present environment the media (TV, Radio, and Newspapers) tend to slant left. Some more and some less. As a young man growing up, I learned to read between the lines. Back then it wasn't as necessary as it is today. Opinions were given on the Op-Ed page and not in the news articles.

That made it easy or at least easier to discern fact from fiction. But today it is just the opposite. As I sit here typing this chapter, I just got done earlier in the day reading at least two articles in the newspaper where the reporters stated a fact then included his/her opinion.

But the opinion was included as though it was a known fact. The undiscerning reader would then file that information away under the category of 'fact'. This leads to confusion.

In fact, I recently stood outside my favorite library waiting for it to open. As I stood there listening to three men discussing America and some of its issues, I heard much misinformation being stated as fact. The statements were sometimes confusing but were obviously gathered from watching too much 'fake news'.

With the left having control of the mainline news, such as TV, radio, and the newspapers, 'fake news' is more predominate than ever and masquerade's as real news. It is no wonder Americans find themselves uninformed.

And this poor reporting has become a major influence upon our youth, who haven't learned to be discerning, and upon older individuals who already have a dim view of the world. It results in misguided actions and causes.

This was never considered good reporting when I was a young man. Back at the end of the 19th Century (no, I wasn't born yet) there was a thing called 'Yellow' journalism. As I recall from my history lessons, that was journalism that was stridently calling for war with Spain! They printed lies, myths, or whatever they could to influence people to subscribe to their view of the world. It was abhorrent and wrong, but they did it anyway.

Back then they didn't have 'fact checkers' so they weren't challenged. You'd hope that today with 'fact checkers' we would learn the truth. But alas that hasn't been the case.

Fact-checkers need to be fact checked themselves. If you must rely upon them, I suggest you use more than one. Even then you can't be sure.

When fact checking first appeared it seemed a good thing, but that is no more a good thing. The left has for the most part taken them over. For shame!

Be Discerning!

So, what can you do?

Do the work yourself.

By that I mean that you do some research. Look up the facts. What happened and what was said to have happened. Fact-checking can be the lazy man's way of getting the truth. When you rely on someone else to do the digging, you are also assuming they have similar biases as you have. Don't assume, find out.

Discernment often requires you to invest in hard work. Choose your fact-checker carefully and back it up with real facts. Fact Checkers are tools that you should use with caution. *But always remember that they are just tools!*

THIRTY-SEVEN : ECONOMY

History

I've been an observer and student of our national and international politics for at least 60 years. I've also paid attention to the economy since it directly affected me. The following is as I recall.

In the year 2008 Barak Obama was elected President of the United States. The recession was already underway by the time he took office. During his tenure of 8 years he tried a variety of ways to right the ship. By the year 2010 experts said the recession was over.

The only problem with that was that people on the bottom of the pay scale up to the middle class didn't notice the ending. I think it is safe to say that the numbers economists followed failed. People with college educations and years of experience in the corporate world were surviving on low paying jobs. But they were jobs and that impacted the numbers.

In addition, people who'd had low paying jobs lost their jobs. They used up their unemployment benefits and still couldn't find a job that would enable them to live at least as comfortable as they once live. But lack of employment over time led to frustration and they stopped seeking employment.

The experts interpreted this to mean that the unemployment had stabilized when in fact it was still in double figures. If I recall correctly it reached the mid-teens.

When Donald Trump announced he was running for the Presidency the economy was still in doldrums. In fact, President Obama, when commenting on the loss of industrial jobs, said that they weren't coming back!

Throughout the election cycle Donald Trump criticized the government for the lack of a real recovery. He made several promises, one of which was to rescind or rewrite the restrictive standards the Obama Administration had decreed. These promises were noticed by businessmen and businesswomen from the small business to the large corporate business. While it is hard to prove since to my knowledge none have spoken about those time, I believe they saw in Trump the necessary relief they needed.

I also suspect that they made contingency plans regarding such questions as: What if Trump kept those promises? What would they mean for their business? What can we do to prepare for such an event without being very public?

In other words, the hope of relief built up the closer to the election we got. Plans were made and safely store away just in case Mr. Trump pulled off what was then considered an impossible upset.

Then came election day November 8, 2016. On that day Donald Trump upset the overconfident Hillary Clinton and won the election! Then while the shocked Democrats cried foul and wouldn't admit to their own failures, the mom and pops suddenly saw that the window of hope had opened.

At the same time the major industry CEOs pulled out those stored plans and activated them. Some plans were futuristic, but some were immediate. And that folks are what I believe the started our economic recovery.

Since then we've seen businesses expand, the hiring of employees growing, real unemployment dip to unheard of depths in decades, and the mom and pop business's started growing again. Oh, by the way the businesses President Obama said would never come back, they're coming back!

What did President Trump do?

NATO

President Trump's speech and actions regarding NATO was widely panned by news reporters. Whether they understood him or not (I doubt they did) they printed and spoke of him in a deprecating manner, questioning his ability to understand international politics.

Predictions of the United States influence waning under President Trump proved to be utterly wrong. Although a few nations were supporting NATO more since 2015, he literally shamed the member nations into increasing their support of NATO. Some nations have promised to do more toward increased funding, others promised more increased military commitment, and some did both. Yet to this day you must really dig to find any mention of this success or acknowledgement that it was his hard-hitting rhetoric and stance that brought it about.

IMPACT on Minorities

President Trump's economic policies has had a positive impact on both the black community and the Latino community. Among other things both now have some of the lowest unemployment numbers of any group within the United States.

Moreover, his tweets regarding Representative Cummings and Baltimore drew widespread condemnation from Black leaders yet drew the support from the overall black community. His poll numbers went from 24% prior to the tweets to 34% after the tweets. And these numbers apparently held true for an entire week!

In fact, despite Democratic candidates bewailing the sorry economy and its unfair impact on the little guy, the testimonies and polls from among these people have gone up. Now the average American, no matter their ethnic heritage, are finding jobs and starting their own businesses. After eight years of a stagnant economy Americans are confident and looking forward to the future.

EXPECTATIONS

I don't make any claims that I'm an economist, but I do have opinions based on years of watching. I believe that when people are comfortable with the direction of the country, they will be more likely to invest and purchased goods. In the case of business, I believe that the confidence of corporate CEOs is extremely high, and these corporate big wigs will continue to expand and hire.

Despite naysayers our economy continues powering forward. And I believe that this will encourage people big and small to invest in their futures. While it may have been the big corporations that made the first steps a lot of smaller businesses, including mom and pop, are also feeling confident that they can expand their business or even start a new business.

The Green New Deal's Impact

You'll find out more about this in the chapter called Green New Deal, but the changes they are talking about would basically restore the restrictive policies of the Obama Administration and impose new taxes upon American business. It would return us to a recession and maybe depression. It is not a *Good Deal*!

THIRTY-EIGHT : FOREIGN RELATIONS

A Personal View

The liberal media, as well as liberal congressional politicians, like to say that Trump is disrespected and considered a laughingstock by world leaders. I have a different view.

When you look at his goals and accomplishments both domestically and internationally you see a man who has achieved a great deal. He didn't do it by being polite or saying 'please'. Rather, he used his position as the President of the United States to force these foreign leaders to bend to his will.

They weren't laughing at him when he threatened to pull out of NATO if they didn't start carrying their fair share of the burden. I didn't see any of them laughing. Rather, they stepped up to the plate and increased both their financial and military assets to NATO.

Our European friends didn't like it when Trump tightened the screws on the Iranians. While it's true that some behind the back deals between them and Iran have been going on, they essentially did nothing. And as tensions have increased, they've gone rather quiet.

The President was rather impolite to the former Prime Minister of Great Britain, but when she was gone the relations between the United States government and Great Britain improved. One commentator called it the beginning of the Anglosphere.

You look around the world today and you see President Trump's brand of diplomacy working wherever he applies it. He understands what it takes to get these foreign leaders to act and he's got the patience to wear them out!

The problem is that our own politicians and the media want a pliable president. They want a president that uses polite words and speaks softly. But he's dealing with strong willed politicians who've been getting their way far too long. So, he plays tough. You may call him a tyrant, a dictator, rude and crude, and ill-mannered, but you certainly can't call him weak or inept. His style works!

Following is a list of foreign accomplishments that President Trump can brag about. I don't pretend they are all listed here, nor do I contend that all controversies or negotiations have been completed. But I do contend that he's amassed quite a record of accomplishments while his erstwhile enemies have been napping.

CHINA

We currently are in a trade war with China. It is true that China is probably the second largest economy in the world. But it is also true that the United States is the largest. If the American people continue to trust President Trump and wait patiently, I believe China will cave.

China has been committing international espionage on the United States for years stealing trade secrets and more. It has plagued the United States for some time including both the Bush and Obama Administrations. But no matter how hard we fought the Chinese they seemed to win. Now President Trump is taking the fight to them.

Is it hurting Americans?

In the case of imports the farmers and others buying goods made in China cost more. But the government has stepped up and is helping. Eventually the Chinese will realize this is a war they cannot win.

Recently I read an article showing the squeeze upon China's economy. It is forcing them to look at different options available to them. One is to cave. Pride prevents them from outright giving in, but I believe that as the squeeze continues, they will come to the table and real progress will take resulting in a reduction in their predatory interactions with other countries' science, product development, and marketing.

The fact is China has only one country where they can sell their merchandise to the extent needed and that's America. On the other hand, the United States has many trading partners. And China knows this reality.

IRAN

When dealing with Iran and its leaders, you are dealing with some very wicked men who aim to make Iran an extremely important member of the world of nations no matter the cost. They are determined to become a nuclear power.

President Obama drew a line in the sand and basically dared them to cross it. They did and he did nothing. President Trump takes a firm stand and they are backing down. Their seizing of ships demonstrates how desperate they are becoming.

Why the difference? Because they always knew how far Obama would or would not go. They don't know what Trump will do!

This causes a lot of handwringing amongst the media and liberal politicians because they don't understand the President's hard line policies. But Trump has been dealing with world leaders for a long time and understands what works for dealing with them.

NAFTA

Canada and Mexico are right on our northern and southern borders. When NAFTA was originally passed our leaders appear to have been outsmarted. In any case, President Trump has been tough on both. First, he played hard with Canada in masterful strategic moves that a chess player would envy. Hard words went back and forth, but it ended with a compromise that gave America a better deal.

Then he turned his attention to Mexico. Where our border with Canada is long and peaceful, the border with Mexico is beset with illegal immigration and smuggling of drugs, etc. It was a different situation but that didn't stop the President. Again, he was able to negotiate a compromise that included Mexico passing and enforcing tough immigration laws.

As a side note the President won a critical court case in the Supreme Court that enables him to use military funds to build the Wall. Also, there's a possibility that Mexico will be paying for the Wall either directly or indirectly.

Are we still friends with these countries? Yes.

NATO

Here's a quote taken from the statement I made in the chapter on the Economy and speaking of NATO: "Predictions of the United States influence waning under President Trump proved to be utterly wrong. Although a few nations were supporting NATO more since 2015, he literally shamed the member nations into increasing their support of NATO. Some nations have promised to do more toward increased funding, others promised more increased military commitment, and some did both. Yet to this day you must really dig to find any mention of this success or acknowledgement that it was his hard-hitting rhetoric and stance that brought it about."

The fact is that although NATO's funding increased three straight years since 2015, most were dragging their feet. By highlighting this Trump was able to get more compliance and promises.

NORTH KOREA

It almost seems unfair to mention North Korea. Trump is the first President to ever meet and negotiate with the North Korean leader. It was historic!

And while there is much yet to do there have been small steps. Of course, back home in the good ole USA the liberals say he's not accomplishing enough. But he's accomplished more than Obama did in eight years! This negotiation is likely to take years, possibly beyond a second term with President Trump. But it is an important negotiation.

RUSSIA

One of the most amazing things has been how Trump has kept Putin in a standstill. If he wanted Trump to be President, as the Democrats claim, then Russia needs to remember 'Beware what you wish for'! During Obama's Presidency Putin pretty much had things his way and that includes the time when Clinton was Secretary of State.

I've listed some of the accomplishments of President Trump versus Putin in the chapter on Trump. Suffice it to say that Trump has been very successful in dealing with Russia.

ANGLOSPHERE

An interesting development is now taking place on the world's political stage. This is what Dick Morris and others call the Anglosphere. It has been coming since at least 2003 and was recently called dead. But it was resurrected before its death was announce. Instead of dying it has impacted both the United Kingdom and the United States. It is a movement that will dominate world politics.

The Anglosphere has centered upon Boris Johnson, the Prime Minister of the United Kingdom, and Donald Trump, President of the United States. These two powerful men lead two of the most powerful countries in the world and seem to have similar views concerning the world's future.

It can be argued that the forces that brought Brexit to the United Kingdom, Boris Johnson to become the Prime Minister, and Donald Trump to the White House are all somewhat related to this Anglosphere. There are other forces as well, but the point is that there is common ground.

Some people argue that the United States and the United Kingdom are losing their influence. I have sincere doubts about that. I think what you are seeing is a moving together of these nations and a moving away from Europe and Asia. Brexit appears to be on the verge of happening despite legal challenges to the Prime Minister's plans.

The very act of moving away from are traditional trading partners will lessen our influence temporarily. But if the Anglosphere becomes a powerful force as some foresee, it's influence would grow. And the Europe/Asian connection will diminish.

So, what is the Anglosphere?

It consists of the United States, United Kingdom, Canada, Australia, New Zealand, India, Ireland, The Bahamas, Barbados, and Jamaica. Some suggest South Africa. They share common cultural and historical ties to the United Kingdom and maintain close political, diplomatic and military cooperation.

With the ascent of Boris Johnson and Brexit you see a move away from the traditional and a move toward other English-speaking nations. This is particularly true of the United Kingdom's move toward the United States.

Both Johnson and Trump are cut from the same populist cloth. They both have entrenched enemies in government and in the media. They have, in my opinion, similar personalities and therefore would understand one another better.

I believe that we are going to see the United States grow closer to the United Kingdom in politics, economics, and diplomacy. That's not to say we don't already have a close relationship, but I think it will grow closer. Not only with the United Kingdom, but with other countries of the Anglosphere.

And that's a good thing!

THIRTY-NINE :IMMIGRATION

Undocumented or Illegal?

The liberals insist on calling immigrants that have violated our laws and entered America 'undocumented immigrants'. Meanwhile, Conservatives call them 'illegal immigrants'.

Let's look at these terms.

Undocumented Immigrants

This term is used to imply that these immigrants are merely missing the proper documentation. It is an argument that undermines the whole idea of documentation.

To understand this better, imagine that instead of immigration the lack of proper documentation affected you as a driver. You've been driving without a license! You'd be punished.

If you were living with someone of the opposite sex without a marriage certificate you could be arrested for adultery.

How about the gun laws which are so precious to liberals? If you owned a gun and didn't have proper documentation, you could be arrested depending on the circumstances.

Documentation is how you determine the legal nature of something.

Illegal Immigrants

This term describes an immigrant that is in the United States illegally. They are required to have a green card or proof of citizenship. It means that they are not citizens, but residents.

In short, if they lack documentation, they are criminals.

And, if they are criminals, they have no more rights than any other criminal. That may seem harsh, but it is reality.

Dreamers

What about children of illegal immigrants?

This is a problem that will be necessary to address sometime soon. The so-called Dream Act is not the answer. But, in my opinion, neither is deportation. I for one would like to see conservatives and liberals sit down and reach a compromise that would solve this issue of children born in America to illegal immigrants. The children deserve this to be resolved.

Some purists argue that providing citizenship to these children is wrong and rewards illegal immigrants. And they have a point. But these children were born in the United States and it wasn't their fault. But here they are.

How about a compromise whereby the children are considered citizens and their parents are given a road that leads to citizenship? Plus, proper consideration of the fact that there are thousands trying to become citizens legally every year.

This is an issue that requires both conservatives and liberals to negotiate in good faith. Don't make it part of a large omnibus bill, but a separate bill that has a chance to be passed.

One last note. When looking at the Issues I purposely used the term the candidates are using, namely 'undocumented'. I believe that since they are using that term a fair representation is to use the same term. It doesn't mean I accept that term.

FORTY : SANCTUARY CITIES

What are they?

One thing I can tell you for sure is that Sanctuary Cities are not the same as the Cities of Refuge found in the Bible. The latter were Biblically designated cities set aside for specific crimes, like manslaughter. There were specific rules and time periods involved. Moreover, in Old Testament times they did not have a court system such as we have today. Yet some people who should know better equate the one with the other.

Since I am not a lawyer, I will provide the Wikipedia explanation of what a Sanctuary City is:

'**Sanctuary city** refers to municipal jurisdictions, typically in North America and Western Europe, that limit their cooperation with the national government's effort to enforce immigration law. Leaders of sanctuary cities say they want to reduce fear of deportation and possible family break-up among people who are in the country illegally, so that such people will be more willing to report crimes, use health and social services, and enroll their children in school. In the United States, municipal policies include prohibiting police or city employees from questioning people about their immigration status and refusing requests by national immigration authorities to detain people beyond their release date, if they were jailed for breaking local law.'

Then comes this statement: the designation "sanctuary city" does not have a precise legal definition.

Like I said, I'm not a lawyer. But I find myself asking how a city can defy national laws? We are not talking about policies here, but of national laws enacted by our Congress. Yet these cities can refuse to enforce the law. How is that possible?

Here is the explanation I found on the Internet:

Most of the focus has been on 8 USC 1373, which says federal, state, or local government entities or officials may not prohibit or restrict the exchange of information with federal immigration officers regarding the citizenship or immigration status of any individual.

A growing number of states, including Florida, have enacted laws that prohibit Sanctuary Cities. This appears to follow the law as stated in 8 USC 1373. Up to now 8 USC 1373 has not been judged by the U.S. Supreme Court. I think the lack of a clear definition guarantees the Supreme Court will eventually have to rule about its constitutionality and the role of states and cities in its enforcement.

The role of the Press

Unfortunately, the Press has decided that we need to be more sensitive to illegal immigrants and call them undocumented immigrants. The very notion demeans the term illegal. Let's be clear, illegal describes something that is contrary to the law.

Someday in the future Christianity will be illegal. By the Press's definition I would be an undocumented worshiper. But, in fact, I would be an illegal worshiper who would be forced to either abandon my faith or face arrest or go in hiding. I won't abandon my faith!

The Press and the liberal politicians who do their bidding have muddied the waters. Another more current comparison is calling wrong that which is right, and right that which is wrong, which we were warned about in the Bible (Judges 17:6, Roman's 1: 18-32, Jude 10-19). Today the reasoning is 'the end justifies the means', which is not only unchristian but exceeding dangerous.

My thought

Protecting the nation's borders is in my opinion the jurisdiction of the Federal Government. If that is the case, then neither a city nor a state can refuse to obey the federal government. The U.S. Supreme Court will have to weigh in on this soon or we'll have rioting in our streets. But I believe the defense of our shores not only refers to military invasion but to any invasion that threatens our nation!

FORTY-ONE : MUELLER INVESTIGATION

History

Although the FBI was investigating the 2016 Primary before the General Election began the intensity and direction of the investigation changed after Donald Trump was elected. If you check with the Fact Checkers, they will tell you there is no evidence of a Deep State or an embedded core of people in the FBI working to undermine the President.

For that reason, it is extremely difficult to know the truth. In the end it appears to be a he said/he said situation. In my opinion, there is enough evidence to at least make an educated guess. For example, there is the Steele Dossier that was used to justify Congress's demand for a Special Counsel, which led to the hiring of Mueller as Special Council.

He was given wide authority, which he used aggressively against Trump's friends, allies, and former employees. Some people were locked up, their homes raided, and underwent rather tough interviewing. Throughout the entire episode President Trump cooperated with the investigation even as his anger grew.

Fast forward and you are now told that the Mueller investigation was successful. But that is untrue. Not a single arrest took place in relation to the primary purpose of the suspected Russian tampering. Those saying it was successful point to the arrest, conviction, and imprisonment of some of Trump's associates. But none of these had anything to do with Russian hacking or tampering.

Actually it appears that the FBI's original investigation unearthed evidence against the Clinton Campaign, but they dropped it suddenly. Questions were raised but apparently never followed up on. And the messy trail left behind by the Steele Dossier doesn't appear to have been investigated.

The result has been itself rather messy. A fair-minded person understands that President Trump has been cleared by the lack of evidence, not because of anything Mueller has said. We live in a country where a person is innocent until proven guilty.

But Mueller left his conclusions hanging so that there would be a cloud hanging over the President's head. This, in turn, left both the Republicans and Democrats angry. The Republicans because the report should have been more conclusive, and Trump presumed innocent; the Democrats because Mueller didn't give them the evidence they wanted and needed to proceed with impeachment.

And Mueller's own reputation suffered because of the "pathetic" testimony he gave regarding the report. About the only thing of value that came from his testimony was the conclusion of others that he wasn't really in charge of the investigation though it bore his name.

It was, in my opinion, a stain on our nation's history. Some people will always believe Trump guilty, while others will always believe Trump innocent. The evidence would seem to favor the latter opinion, but it is unlikely we'll ever know the truth.

The Report

The report is quite long. I was recently in the bookstore and saw the book. It was extremely thick. But those who have read honestly and without malice come up with two conclusions:

1) Collusion between the Trump Campaign and Russia could not be proven and wasn't likely.
2) Obstruction of Justice could not be proven because a) a crime was never determined to have happened, and b) there is no evidence that Trump ever engaged in tampering with the investigation though he may have wanted to do so.

Understanding there is a lot of legalize involved in understanding this issue I will use a question and answer approach to this.

Question: **What was the conclusion about Collusion?**

Answer:

The Mueller team left that unanswered. But after two years and millions of dollars we deserve better than an unanswered question. It would seem to me that if the investigation ended without enough evidence to make a charge then the answer is no collusion. There simply wasn't any real evidence that collusion ever took place.

Were there contacts between the Trump Campaign and Russia?

It appears so, but at the same time those contacts led to nothing. Which is a whole lot better than what apparently happened between the Clintons and Russia. That's another issue and we won't explore that here.

So, while liberals say Trump wasn't proved innocent, that isn't the question. We live in a country where you are innocent until proven guilty and he wasn't proved guilty at all!

Which raises another question. If there was no crime (collusion) how can you have obstruction of justice? And exactly what is obstruction of justice?

Here's a legal explanation:

"... the crime or act of willfully interfering with the process of **justice** and law especially by influencing, threatening, harming, or impeding a witness, potential witness, juror, or judicial or legal officer or by furnishing false information in or otherwise impeding an investigation or legal process the defendant's ..."

The so-called evidence in this (assuming you are pursuing this charge) is no evidence at all. Let's see, Trump was angry and told someone that it must not happen. Did he do something wrong?

No!

Did the President fire Mueller?

No!

Did the President fire Comey?

Yes, after the investigation was over.

Is any of this 'High Crimes and Misdemeanors'?

No!

Does this episode indicate people within the Justice Department want to get rid of President Trump? That needs to be examined. The Attorney General should investigate his Department and root out anyone guilty of such crimes. And if he can't get it done, then involve the Congress.

There is one thing in this whole mess that is obvious. The Democrats have embarrassed themselves. They so wanted to prove President

Trump guilty of something that they refused to give up even when the investigator failed to deliver the evidence. And not only Democrats share in this guilt. Some Republicans, current and past, aided in encouraging this investigation, including the use of the contrived Steele Dossier, which a simple reading should have raised their suspicions.

There is another thing that is obvious. The Mueller team went to great lengths to uncover a crime and failed to do so. They used tactics that were quite extraordinary, including using solitary confinement as an investigative tool. Such crudeness alarms me and should alarm all Americans! Yes, he did discover crimes by people who Trump did business with, but does that justify the methods used?

The Impact

What will be the impact of the Mueller report?

In my opinion, the Mueller report only solidifies people's existing opinions. If you're against Donald Trump in the beginning, you'll excuse the lack of evidence and believe that President Trump did something wrong and is going to get away with it. And it angers you!

If you believe this is all nothing but a witch hunt, then you reject the entire collusion charge and insist on his innocence. To be honest, I've read articles from people on either side and the ones convicting Trump have a consistent theme: Trump is guilty because we 'know' he's capable of such wickedness and therefore must have done it. Yet they only offer supposition as facts!

The only impact I've seen comes in four statements:

Statement One: The Report has stimulated divisiveness instead of answering innocence or guilt. The country is divided!

Statement Two: Millions and Billions of dollars have been wasted on this Report with nothing to show for it.

Statement Three: This Report has virtually paralyzed both houses of Congress, so real issues have gone unresolved.

Statement Four: This Report has occupied the White House and the Administration to the degree that their focus has been divided, thereby limiting their effectiveness.

FORTY-TWO : GREEN NEW DEAL

On February 7, 2019 Representative Cortez teamed up with Senator Markey and released a fourteen-page resolution for what they called the Green New Deal. According to *The Washington Post* article published on February 11th they are calling for a "10-year national mobilization" with the following primary goals (as I've summarized):

- Guaranteed job with a family-sustaining wage, including family and medical leave, paid vacations and retirement security for all
- High quality health care
- affordable, safe, and adequate housing.
- Economic security
- Clean water and Clean air
- Healthy and affordable food, and nature
- Providing Resources, training, and high-quality education, including higher education
- Meet 100% of the country's power demand by using clean, renewable, and zero-emission energy sources
- Repair and upgrade our infrastructure
- Eliminating pollution and greenhouse gas emissions.
- Building/upgrading buildings to energy-efficient, distributed, and smart power grids
- Overhauling transportation systems to eliminate pollution and greenhouse gas emissions
- Investing (code word for tax supported) zero-emission vehicle infrastructure
- Manufacturing clean, affordable, and accessible public transportation and high-speed rail.

All of this will spur massive growth in clean manufacturing and removing pollution and greenhouse gas emissions from manufacturing and industry as much as is technologically feasible. The plan also includes working with farmers and ranchers to eliminate pollution and greenhouse gas emissions from the agricultural sector as much as is technologically feasible.

Their goal is for the United States to use 100% renewable, zero-emission energy sources including electric cars, high-speed rail and implementing the "social cost of carbon" that was part of the Obama administration's plan.

My Analysis

It looks to me that the following was added to make it even more appealing: universal health care, higher minimum wages, and the prevention of monopolies.

It does not take a genius or even a person well acquainted with the industries affected to see what this would do to America. In short, this plan would reduce America to a third world country. Industries overburdened with excessive taxes will either relocate to other countries or go out of business. This in turn would lead to massive unemployment worse than what we recently experienced.

This Green New Deal is no deal at all. It's supporters claim that it will be adequately funded by higher taxes on the rich, but there is not enough money out there to accomplish their goals.

One of the most interesting and baffling things that's existed for decades is that the so-called party of the workers has an abundance of wealthy people supporting it, including many of the Democrats running for office. Are we to believe they're willing to lose almost all their wealth to bring about this transformation?

It was wealthy men who gave their lives, property, and wealth to establish this country. So, is it reasonable to assume these wealthy men and women are willing to make the same sacrifice? I think not, but I could be wrong.

Are their goals desirable? Some for sure. But the naïve approach they are advocating would bring about a desolate country that I would not want to be living in. I am not a millionaire or anywhere close to it, but I would like to have the opportunity to have more money. Do I want it for my own self-aggrandizement? For a more comfortable living? Sure. But primarily I want to do more to get the Gospel out, to help my own church and other churches, to support missions more than I currently do, and to help other people who have needs.

But this 'Deal' would have a negative impact upon my career and the careers of millions of people! It simply is nothing more than a wish list to be paid for by others.

I asked earlier if these people would be willing to lose everything for their cause. I said that 'I think not'. Some of them gained their wealth outside of government service and some gained their wealth through their government service. It is extremely hard to believe that people who labored and took advantage of every break they could find to get their capitalistic gains will willingly give it all up.

To be honest, I find it difficult to believe that AOC and her cohorts are really that naïve that they fail to see the weakness of their plans. For instance, if you've been around for any length of time you've probably heard of government or private industry speaking of reaching individual goals within so many years. And you've also seen that these goals for the most part didn't materialize as planned.

That's because things hardly ever move as fast as we want. During the Obama years the administration tried to achieve certain goals pertaining to protecting natural resources. They probably had good intentions, but they ran into resistance. From the rich? Not at all; it came from the farmers and property owners. It required unexpected amounts of money and time for the government to achieve any progress. And a lot of anger!

If those efforts had continued beyond Obama's presidency it might someday have been achieved but at terrific cost!

The only successful effort to reach a desired goal in record time that I'm aware of was the government's response to the Soviet Union's space program. President Kennedy launched an ambitious program to eventually surpass the Soviets and eventually we did. But that program was costly, involved major investments by industry, and dedication by both professionals and non-professionals. It succeeded because the same people who'd be hurt by this new plan dedicated themselves to the success of the Space Program!

When I look at their Green New Deal, I see a bleak world, shuttered plants, desolate streets, and millions of homeless. The rush to implement this plan will run roughshod over both the rich and the poor. The Middle Class will disappear with most becoming poor. Some of the rich will get richer because they know how to work hard and gain, no matter what the financial conditions are.

In the end America as we know it will be history! And you and I will be living in its ashes!

FORTY-THREE : THE SQUAD

An Opinion

While none of these women are running to become President, their radical ideas are changing the Democratic Party and the political landscape.

It began simple enough. Four congresswomen-elect (Alexandria Ocasio Cortez, Ilhan Omar, Rashida Tlaid, and Ayanna Pressley) met in Washington in November 2018 for new member orientation. A snapshot was taken of them gathered together for an interview.

Cortez (aka AOC) suggested it be titled #squadgoals. It wasn't long before it was shortened to Squad.

As the Primary has continued the Squad has become identified with divisional politics. In July, President Trump tweeted they should go back to their own country.

This tweet was taken out of context (in this case, the radicalism and unpatriotic nature of the women) to represent racism. While all four are citizens they publicly denounced America which was the obvious reference Trump was trying to emphasize. His tweet said nothing about color, race, etc. although almost every news article about the tweet points out they are women of color and none that I've read have said a thing about their anti-Semitic, racist, and/or anti-American rants. (One note: the anti-Semitism was commented upon in at least one article.)

The result has been feigned outrage by the media and Democrats. How effective their outrage is will be seen as the primary goes forward. Early returns from polls have shown Trump's approval rating rising not falling.

One reason why the President's approval has gone higher might be that the public realizes the outrage is contrived. It is also apparent that the Squad's criticisms are largely at odds with the facts concerning the economy, civil rights, and more.

Another factor indicates that the Democratic Party itself is embarrassed by the hatred and lies that emanate from their mouths.

Some of these have been recorded for all to see and hear. Once the general election takes place it is altogether possible that the Republican Party will successfully wrap the Squad around the Party Nominee and therefore undercut that Nominee's campaign.

As I've stated the whole outrage strikes me and millions of Americans to be contrived. The whole idea is to make the President look like a racist, although his personal and Presidential policies have improved the lives of all Americans no matter what their color. It's further my opinion that they've failed because the American people are very discerning.

~

REVIEW REQUESTED

Dear Reader,

If you enjoyed the *2020 Election Candidates & Issues*, why not review it? I provide free copies (PDF or EPUB) for honest reviews.

How do I review the book?

Simple. Use a rating of 1 to 5 with 1 the lowest and 5 the highest. Then simply give a detailed reason for the rating.

Here are the steps:

- Read the book.
- Rate the book.
- Give detailed reason for the rating.
- Post.
- Let me know

If you do review the book on Amazon, I thank you in advance. Your opinion is important to me. It will help potential readers to decide and it will help me to become a better writer.

To contact me (R. Frederick Riddle) simply send an email to marketing@tr-indbkstore.com with "Book Review of [title]" in the subject line. Be sure to indicate desired format of book.

R. Frederick Riddle loved writing long before publishing his first book in 2003. Over the years he has established himself as a writer of Bible based books. While not all are Bible based this has been his forte.

A student of the Bible as well as a student of writing, he has now written three books of the *World That Was* series (*Perished, World of Noah and the Ark, World of Shem,* and *World of Abraham*). To inquire about his books or to comment on his books he can be reached at his Facebook Business page which is at *https://www.facebook.com/RFrederickRiddlesWorld/* or on Twitter at *AuthorRiddle.*

BOOKS BY R. FREDERICK RIDDLE

The author and his wife Teresa (aka Tress) are co-founders of T&R Independent Books.

NON-FICTION

➢2020 Election Candidates and Issues
So You Want To Write

FICTION

The World That Was series
- Perished (volume 1)
- World of Noah and the Ark (volume 2)
- World of Shem (volume 3)
- World of Abraham (volume 4)
- World of Jacob (volume 5)

Christland series
- Death Ship(Book 1)
- A New Home (Book 2)
- Task Force! (Book 3)
- Black Death (Book 4)
- Rise of I.C.E.S. (Book 5)
- Battle at Proxima Centauri (Book 6)

Watch for Tess Riddle's debut novel.

T&R Independent Books is the publisher of books by R. Frederick Riddle and Tess Riddle.

www.ingramcontent.com/pod-product-compliance
Lightning Source LLC
Chambersburg PA
CBHW051445250726
48655CB00001B/250